THE TEXT OF
GULLIVER'S TRAVELS

THE SANDARS LECTURES
IN BIBLIOGRAPHY
1950

THE TEXT OF
GULLIVER'S TRAVELS

BY

SIR HAROLD WILLIAMS

CAMBRIDGE
AT THE UNIVERSITY PRESS
1952

CAMBRIDGE UNIVERSITY PRESS
Cambridge, New York, Melbourne, Madrid, Cape Town,
Singapore, São Paulo, Delhi, Mexico City

Cambridge University Press
The Edinburgh Building, Cambridge CB2 8RU, UK

Published in the United States of America by Cambridge University Press, New York

www.cambridge.org
Information on this title: www.cambridge.org/9781107623545

First published 1952
First paperback edition 2013

A catalogue record for this publication is available from the British Library

ISBN 978-1-107-62354-5 Paperback

CONTENTS

v

PREFACE

If Swift cannot be credited with being a careful proof-reader, nor, like his friend Pope, a sedulous reviser, he took more trouble with his writings, on occasion, than is supposed. Unfortunately *Gulliver's Travels*, the best known to the general reader of all his works, was left to the arbitrary handling of a London bookseller. When the printed work, unseen beforehand, reached Swift, he was moved to protest against liberties which had been taken with his manuscript. In despite, however, the book has, for generations, been read by many in a text marred by unauthorised perversions.

It is less than thirty years since the first close and searching investigation of the textual problem of *Gulliver's Travels* appeared. Conclusions then reached have been called in question; and a further examination is now justified.

I am grateful to Lord Rothschild for permission to make full use of the 1727–32 Pope and Swift *Miscellanies* in his possession. These volumes contain many corrections in Swift's hand. The adoption of these corrections by Faulkner, the Dublin bookseller, in his editions of Swift's poems and miscellaneous writings, lends authority, as I have striven to show, to his revised text of *Gulliver's Travels*.

H.W.

December 1951

I. THE PUBLICATION OF
GULLIVER'S TRAVELS

It has been said, and, in my opinion, without undue exaggeration, that Swift's writings 'bristle with editorial difficulties as complex as any in the whole range of English literature'.[1] I may, therefore, be forgiven for occupying myself in these lectures with an author to whom I have devoted many years of study without exhausting, by any means, all that may be said bibliographically and textually about his writings. Within the bounds of bibliography and text I hope to confine myself, so far as I can control any tendency to stray.

Not long after the war of 1914–18, when demobilized, I entered by a chance for which I can call to mind no prompting the shop of J. and J. Leighton, antiquarian booksellers of high standing in their day, though now for many years only a memory of the past. I bought, again for no reason that I can remember, two of the 1726 editions of *Gulliver's Travels*. I had not then any special interest in Swift; but in life it is only the unexpected that happens. At home I began to turn over the pages of the four volumes I had purchased, and

[1] Émile Pons in *The Review of English Studies*, xxv, 364.

before long it was borne in upon me that here was a bibliographical problem calling for solution. I ransacked the shelves of booksellers. I read their catalogues. Soon more and more editions of *Gulliver* lined my own shelves. The problem began to clear itself; and I, who had never previously given much of my time to the minutiae of bibliography or textual research, succeeded, I hope, in teaching myself some guiding principles.

In 1926, the bicentenary of the publication of *Gulliver's Travels*, I brought out an edition following the first text, although I maintained in my introduction that the Dublin version, published by George Faulkner in 1735, represented Swift's last thoughts and was nearer to the original manuscript from which, with excisions and alterations, Benjamin Motte printed the first edition in London. It was not until I was well forward with my work that I came upon *Contributions towards a Bibliography of Gulliver's Travels*, 1922, by an American scholar, Lucius L. Hubbard. To his work and to correspondence with him I make grateful acknowledgement. We had independently ranged ourselves on the side of Faulkner. This preference has met with general acceptance. In the Shakespeare Head edition of Swift's *Prose Works*, for example, in which Dr Herbert Davis gives special attention to the text, *Gulliver's Travels* follows the Faulkner version.

On what grounds have I any excuse to-day for returning to a problem with which I occupied myself a quarter of a century ago? There are good reasons. Otherwise I should not have presumed to invite your patient attention in these lectures. The first reason is that it has now become necessary to examine afresh the textual claims of Faulkner versus Motte, since the late Professor Arthur E. Case published in 1938 an edition of *Gulliver*[1] based on the first edition of 1726 corrected from a list of errata sent to the publisher in 1727 by Charles Ford, a friend of Swift, and further amended by the insertion of passages of some length written out on blank leaves by Ford in his own copy of the first edition of the work. Case summarily adjudged Swift's part in affording any revisional assistance to Faulkner as 'perfunctory'. In 1945 he returned to the charge,[2] justifying at much greater length the text he had adopted in 1938, and belittling the textual value of Faulkner's edition. Professor Case was possessed of an acute and original mind; he had the gift of marshalling evidence; his argument was conducted in terms courteous and persuasive; he succeeded in awakening doubts and winning some converts.

A second good reason for returning to *Gulliver* in these lectures will, however, lead us to a restate-

---

[1] New York, Thomas Nelson and Sons, 1938.
[2] *Four Essays on 'Gulliver's Travels'* .... Princeton, 1945

ment of the story of the publication of the work before we come to an examination of the text. Since my edition appeared in 1926 and that of Dr Herbert Davis in 1941, accompanied by an introduction from my pen, new facts have been brought to light by Dr H. Teerink, to whose paper[1] on the subject I make full acknowledgement. I shall here avoid, so far as is possible, any repetitive account of the negotiations leading to the publication of *Gulliver's Travels*, confining myself to corrections and additions, and the deductions which may be drawn from new manuscript material.

We know that Swift began to put the work together about the end of 1720 or the beginning of 1721. It was completed and revised during the summer of 1725. He was in London by about the middle of March 1726 carrying the manuscript. He visited old friends and spent a considerable time with Pope at Twickenham. Early in August he was back in London, apparently staying with John Gay at his lodgings in Whitehall. Not until his return to town, five months after his arrival in England, were any steps taken to approach a publisher. Then a letter clearly of Swift's composition, though not in his hand, dated 8 August 1726, and signed with the fictitious name 'Richard Sympson', was dropped secretively at the house of Benjamin Motte, accom-

[1] 'The Publication of *Gulliver's Travels*', *Dublin Magazine*, January 1948, pp. 14–27.

4

panied by part of the manuscript of *Gulliver's Travels*. 'Richard Sympson', professing himself Lemuel Gulliver's cousin, submits for consideration in abridged form his relative's Travels, in the belief that 'they will sell very well', and asks for the return of the 'Papers', if rejected, 'in three Days at furthest'. The least that he will accept for publication rights is £200, which he intends to put to 'the use of poor Sea-men'. Motte is informed that if he agrees to the terms he may begin to print forthwith, 'and the subsequent parts shall be all sent to you one after another in less than a week', provided that within three days he delivers a bank bill for £200 to a special messenger who will call. If he does not approve the proposal he is asked to return the papers by the special messenger or by means of his own.

It will be agreed that the average publisher might well be repelled, if not incensed, by an approach from an unknown author so unbending and unconciliatory. It speaks volumes for Motte's judgement that he accepted the manuscript at once. We may, of course, readily believe that almost from the first he suspected the identity of the author. The draft of his reply is undated; but it may be presumed to have been written on 11 August, the day on which the messenger was to call for an answer. He accepted the proposal made him, and offered to publish within a month of receipt of copy; but he asked that a promise to pay the £200 within six months should be trusted, for he could not immediately deposit 'so considerable a Sum'. The laconic reply of the fictitious 'Sympson' is dated 13 August: 'I would have both Volumes come out together and published by Christmas at furthest.' These three letters have been known for some time, for they were printed in *The Gentleman's Magazine* in 1856.[1] They represent all that has been preserved of the negotiations with Motte prior to publication.

Until recently we were dependent upon *The Gentleman's Magazine* for our knowledge of the letters. Dr F. Elrington Ball, in his edition of Swift's *Correspondence*,[2] took his text directly from that publication. To Dr Teerink belongs the credit of drawing attention to the originals of these letters in the Pierpont Morgan Library, New York.[3] They had come into the possession of the Rev. Charles Bathurst Woodman, and were by him communicated to *The Gentleman's Magazine*, in which periodical they were printed in conventionalized form, and inaccurately in the case of the second letter. This mistake need not here detain us.

At this stage two questions calling for resolution present themselves: (a) Was the manuscript sub-

[1] N.S. xliv, 34–6.

[2] *The Correspondence of Jonathan Swift* (1910–14), iii, 328–31, subsequently cited as *Corresp.*

[3] Dr Maxwell B. Gold noted the presence of the letters in the Pierpont Morgan Library, but carried the matter no further. *Swift's Marriage to Stella*, pp. 178–9.

mitted to Motte in Swift's hand or was it a transcript? (*b*) Who was the bearer of the letter
addressed to Motte accompanying the manuscript?

(*a*) Professor F. P. Wilson's pronouncement:[1]
'The most important contribution that critical
bibliography has made to the textual criticism of
Shakespeare is its insistence upon the importance
of discovering all that can be known or inferred
about the manuscript from which the printer set
up his copy, and all that can be known or inferred
about what happened to the manuscript in the
printing-house' is of general import and not confined
to Shakespearean studies. We can infer within
close limits the text of the manuscript received by
Motte. Was it, however, Swift's holograph, or was
it a transcript?

It is curious that, as Swift was in England for
five months in 1726, active negotiations with the
publisher occupied only a few days at the very end
of his visit before he left for Ireland. What was
happening to the manuscript of *Gulliver* all this
time? There is some indication, and much probability, that the manuscript was shown to several
friends, Pope, Gay, and Ford especially, and that
suggestions thereupon were made. Additions,
deletions, and alterations may have followed.
Possibly also a transcript was made. This would
take time, for the work runs to about 120,000

[1] *Studies in Retrospect* (Bibliographical Society), p. 124.

7

words. A transcript at this stage need only be presumed if the manuscript Swift brought with him from Ireland was in his own hand. Sympson's first letter to Motte admitted that 'some parts of this and the following Volumes may be thought in one or two places to be a little Satyrical, yet in general they will give no Offence, but in that you must judge for your self, and take the Advice of your Friends, and if they or you be of another opinion, you may let me know it when you return these Papers'. In other words Swift realized that some of the political allusions of the narrative might well be considered dangerous. It is probable, therefore, that, in default of proper safeguards, he would be unwilling to allow his holograph to go forward. We know that on previous occasions he adopted a similar precaution. When in 1714 he com-missioned Charles Ford to negotiate publication of his pamphlet, *Some Free Thoughts upon the Present State of Affairs*, he instructed him to get 'some Friend to copy out the little Paper' and to send it to the printer by an unknown hand.[1] He was careful to send abroad in another hand the *Drapier's Letters*, which attacked the English government's administration of Irish affairs. Swift's general practice with writings politically dangerous suggests that a transcript was delivered to Motte. Dr Teerink holds that the question is not in doubt. He quotes

[1] *Letters of Swift to Ford*, ed. D. Nichol Smith, p. xxi.

8

from a letter written by Swift from London,
7 July 1726, to Thomas Tickell, then in Dublin
as secretary to the Lord Lieutenant:

'As to what you mention of an imaginary treatise,
I can only answer that I have a great quantity of
papers somewhere or other, of which none would
please you, partly because they are very incorrect,
but chiefly because they wholly disagree with your
notions of persons and things; neither do I believe
it would be possible for you to find out my treasury
of waste papers, without searching nine houses, and
then sending to me for the key.'[1]

On the next day Swift wrote to his friend
Thomas Sheridan:

'Our friend at the Castle [Tickell] writ to me
two months ago to have a sight of those papers, etc.,
of which I brought away a copy. I have answered
him, that whatever papers I have are conveyed
from one place to another through nine or ten hands,
and that I have the key. If he should mention anything of papers in general, either to you or the ladies,
and that you can bring it in, I would have you and
them to confirm the same story, and laugh at my
humour in it, etc.'[2]

It is true that in the second letter Swift speaks of
'a copy'; but the word should not be taken in too
exact a sense, or as we might commonly use it to-day.
For two hundred years before the time at which
Swift was writing, the word 'copy' ordinarily

[1] *Corresp.* iii, 314. [2] *Ib.* iii, 316.

9

denoted an individual example of a manuscript. His object was to put off the Whig secretary of a Whig Viceroy with a fantastic story of innumerable papers scattered in nine repositories. Does he not himself refer to the 'humour in it'? In this connexion the word cannot be interpreted to settle beyond question the fact that Swift carried with him from Ireland a transcript of *Gulliver* done by another hand. Nine months earlier, 29 September 1725, Swift wrote to Pope:

'I have employed my time, besides ditching, in finishing, correcting, amending, and transcribing my Travels, in four parts complete . . . and intended for the press.'[1]

Here Swift speaks of a transcript in his own hand, a transcript 'intended for the press'. From this passage it might be argued with much greater force than the contrary deduction from the story invented for Tickell's benefit, that the manuscript Swift carried with him to England was in his own hand. But it would be unsafe to assume as much; for Swift's words need not be taken as meaning more than the casting and writing out of his *Travels* in the final form intended for publication. A transcript in another hand might well have followed, before he started for England five months later. Whichever way we turn we get no certain help. Faulkner in his 'Advertisement' to the 1735 edition of the

[1] *Corresp.* iii, 276.

Travels says: 'We are assured, that the Copy sent to the Bookseller in London, was a Transcript of the Original.' In the same volume, however, in a new preface composed by Swift, entitled 'A Letter from Capt. Gulliver to his Cousin Sympson' we read: 'And I hear the original Manuscript is all destroyed, since the Publication of my Book. Neither have I any Copy left.' This might be taken to imply that the author's holograph was used by the printer, and that there was no transcript to take its place. It must be remembered, however, that the 'Letter' was part of an imaginary narrative. In any event the words, 'original Manuscript', would not mean for Swift what at a glance we should take them to mean. At a later date we find him, for example, describing a copy of the *Four Last Years of the Queen* in the hand of an amanuensis, as 'the originall Manuscript of the History, corrected by me'.[1] Thus, on the evidence so far recounted, we could not be certain that a transcript of the *Travels* was made, although, on the knowledge we have of Swift's habits, this seems probable.

If we pursue the matter further, however, there is some indication of the possibility that the manuscript was Swift's last revision in his own hand, made in Ireland, and that the publisher was enjoined to destroy it when printing was complete. When destroyed identification of the author would

[1] *The Library*, xvi, 87.

be difficult. In 1733, when Swift was in correspondence with Ford about a new and revised
edition of the *Travels* to be published in Dublin, he
seems to have taken it for granted that the manuscript used by Motte was no longer extant.[1] As we
have seen, the same assumption is to be found in the
'Letter from Capt. Gulliver to his Cousin Sympson'
prefixed to Faulkner's edition. Further, when
in 1727 Motte brought out a so-called 'Second
Edition' of the *Travels*, corrected in conformity with
a list of errors furnished him by Charles Ford, he did
not make use of a manuscript, for it is clear that he
set up the new edition from a copy of the first edition
of 1726 containing the original D8 in Vol. ii,
subsequently replaced by a cancel leaf. This does
in some measure, but by no means conclusively,
suggest that the printer, when faced with the
problem of embodying Ford's corrections, was no
longer able to turn to the manuscript to see what he
could do about it. On the other hand two of Ford's
caustic comments in the list he sent to the printer[2]
read as if he took it for granted that reference to the
manuscript was possible.

We are thus left without any certain answer to
the question—Was the manuscript sent to the printer
in Swift's hand, or was it a transcript? Textually
the point is not of first-rate importance, for Swift was

[1] *Letters of Swift to Ford*, ed. D. Nichol Smith, pp. 153–5.
[2] *Gulliver's Travels*, ed. Harold Williams, pp. 423–31.

careful in these matters, and the transcript, if there was one, would accurately represent his final revision.

(*b*) I turn now to the question—Who carried the Sympson letter and part of the manuscript to the printer's house? Hitherto two of Swift's friends have been competitors for the place of honour, Charles Ford and Erasmus Lewis. A third, John Gay, carrying strong credentials, now enters the field.[1]

Sir Walter Scott, in his *Memoirs of Swift* (1814, p. 326), discussing the publication of *Gulliver's Travels*, states categorically in a footnote that 'Charles Ford, formerly employed in the negociation with Barber, about the "Free Thoughts"... rendered this second piece of secret service to the Dean'. In the introduction to his edition of the *Letters of Swift to Ford*, p. xxi, Professor Nichol Smith takes up this clue, observing:

'We do not know what evidence Scott had, but if he had less than we have, we should say that he guessed shrewdly. He mentions the part that Ford had played in conveying to the printer *Some Free Thoughts upon the Present State of Affairs* in 1714; but he did not know, as we now do, what instructions Ford had then received from Swift:

"Here it is, read it, and send it to B—— by an unknown hand....Do not send it by the Penny post, nor your Man, but by a Porter when you are

---

[1] Pope, who has been named, was not at the critical time in London.

not at your Lodgings. Get some Friend to copy out the little Paper, and send it enclosed with the rest, and let the same Hand direct it, and seal it with an unknown Seal."

Nor did Scott know that Swift had drafted a letter to be addressed to the printer of *Free Thoughts*, and to be printed before the pamphlet. It is the same technique. We cannot bring conclusive proof, but, as we shall see, Ford was in the secret of *Gulliver* at every stage.'

It must be remembered, however, that these plans antedate *Gulliver* by twelve years. We should be cautious in allowing them too much weight. Furthermore, on the likely presumption that Swift knew in August 1726 that Ford would be leaving London in a few weeks, he might have been influenced to choose as his secret negotiator some one who could be trusted to remain in or near London until the publication of the work. In a letter addressed to Pope and Gay, written from Dublin in the earlier half of October 1726, Swift says: 'Mr Ford is just landed, after a month's raking by the way.'¹ Even if we do not take Swift's 'month' too literally this implies that Ford left London by the middle of September at the latest; and it is at least probable that Swift would have preferred to arrange for one negotiator to treat with Motte from the first approach until publication.

¹ *Coresp.* iii, 350.

Erasmus Lewis can claim documentary evidence in his favour. In 1733–4 Motte consulted him in consequence of action taken by the government against those implicated in the publication of Swift's poem, *Epistle to a Lady*.[1] In other words he looked to Lewis both as a friend and an agent of Swift. Later, 1737–8, Lewis had a large part to play during proposals for the publication of Swift's *Four Last Years of the Queen*. Further, he had a direct, if late, part in the secret negotiations with Motte conducted under the fictitious name of 'Sympson', not in connexion with the publication of *Gulliver*, but with the payment of £200. The letter reads:

'Mr Motte

I sent this enclosed by a friend to be sent to you, to desire that you would go to the House of Erasmus Lewis Esqr in Cork-street behind Burlington house, and let him know that you are come from me. for the sd Mr Lewis I have given full power to treat with you concerning my Cozn Gulliver's book and what ever he & you shall settle I will consent to so I have written to him You will see him best early in the morning

I am yr humble Servant

Richd Sympson'

Apr. 27th 1727

[1] *Corresp.* v, 215; *Poems of Swift*, ed. H. Williams, p. 629.

This letter is endorsed in Lewis's hand:

> 'London. may. 4. 1727
> I am fully satisfyd. E. Lewis'[1]

Here we find Lewis handling a 'Sympson' letter, acting as Swift's business agent, collecting the agreed payment stipulated in an earlier 'Sympson' letter for the publication rights of *Gulliver's Travels*. This is not conclusive evidence that he was also the bearer of the earlier Sympson letters, but he was a trusted friend of Swift's of long standing, he resided a large part of his time in London; and he would, therefore, be as useful, as reliable, and as readily available a go-between as could well be found. Dr Teerink's off-hand pronouncement that 'there is not a scrap of evidence, or even of proba-bility, to prove that he had anything to do with *Gulliver* at this early stage', and that he can 'safely be dismissed', is a hasty over-statement.[2]

A clue to the very likely probability of a third friend having been the bearer of the first 'Sympson' letter and of a sample portion of the *Gulliver* manuscript is provided in a letter written from London to Swift by John Gay on 22 October 1726, that is six days before the publication of the *Travels*. The importance of this letter seems to have

[1] Original in the Pierpont Morgan Library. I agree with Dr Teerink that it does appear to have been written by Swift himself in a deliberately disguised hand.
[2] *Dublin Magazine* (January 1948), p. 23.

been missed by previous commentators. The letter opens:

'Before I say one word to you, give me leave to say something of the other gentleman's affair. The letter was sent, and the answer was, that everything was finished and concluded according to orders, and that it would be publicly known to be so in a very few days, so that, I think, there can be no occasion for his writing any more about this affair.'[1]

The reference can only be to negotiations with the publisher. The letter makes it clear that (*a*) more correspondence with Motte had taken place than is preserved to us; and that (*b*) Gay was at the centre of the negotiations.

We can now turn back to the two letters of 8 and 13 August 1726, and ask—Can the handwriting be identified? Here I find myself in agreement with Dr Teerink that they are both in the hand of Gay.[2] On a comparison of the letter of 8 August with several examples of Gay's hand the first instinct is one of some hesitation. A close examination, how- ever, makes it clear that although Gay adopted a precise and formal script of set purpose, giving to the page an angularity unlike his normal habit, letter formations typically his are so constant that no doubt can be entertained. In the brief letter of 13 August no concealment is attempted. The hand

[1] *Corresp.* iii, 351.
[2] *Dublin Magazine* (January 1948), pp. 18–19.

is that of Gay. It is a tempting but by no means an inescapable conclusion that Gay was both copyist and bearer of the 'Sympson' letters. Furthermore, allusions in surviving correspondence between Swift, Pope, and Gay, in the interval of ten weeks and four days between Swift's departure from London (15 August) and the publication of *Gulliver's Travels* (28 October) show that two or more letters have been lost, and that during September Gay, who was 'upon the ramble'[1] in the country with the Duke and Duchess of Queensberry, handed over transactions with Motte to Pope.[2] Thus both Ford and Gay were out of town at about the same time. Gay, however, was soon back, remained there, and was in touch with Motte during the period of publication, as we know from his letter of 22 October.[3]

On the other hand, an argument which may be regarded as telling against the likelihood of Gay appearing in person for the conduct of negotiations, at least in the early stages, is that the secrecy Swift sought might have been endangered. Motte may well have heard that Swift was lodging with Gay. If the printer recognized the handwriting or the

[1] 16 Sept. *Corresp*. iii, 340.

[2] Gay to Swift, 16 Sept. *Corresp*. iii, 341: 'As for the particular affair that you want to be informed in, we are as yet wholly in the dark; but Mr. Pope will follow your instructions.'

[3] *Corresp*. iii, 351.

bearer himself, the secret would be out. This could hardly have escaped Swift's thoughts; and thus might have led him to choose another messenger. However far this may appear to stray into idle speculation, it is, at least, proper to suppose that as it occurs to us it might have occurred to Swift.

It has not been possible to decide with certainty that the manuscript of Swift's work received by Motte was a transcript in another hand. I believe that it was. If we take account of Swift's habitual practice when sending to a printer documents of doubtful political implication we may be fairly well assured that the copy for *Gulliver* was a transcript. However, a doubt remains; and certainly a doubt as to the bearer of the 'Sympson' letter. This may be disappointing; but it is better to accept uncertainties, when one must, rather than to persuade ourselves into doubtful beliefs which may lead us astray in bibliographical or textual judgements.

I have occupied myself with these two matters because there was something new to be said. So far as Motte's edition of *Gulliver's Travels* is concerned we are on generally known and accepted ground. The work proved a 'best seller'. Three octavo editions with Motte's imprint appeared in 1726. A duodecimo appeared in 1727, and an octavo in the same year. The 1727 octavo is textually important. It was, as has been shown already, set up from a first issue of the first edition. Certain errors or changes which had crept into the second octavo were followed in the third octavo and in the duodecimo. Motte went back to the first octavo as containing a more accurate text, deriving directly from the author's manuscript, for he intended at the same time a larger revision in consequence of a complaint he had received, written from Dublin, 3 January 1727, by Charles Ford, alleging that the printed book abounded 'with many gross Errors of the Press'. Continuing, Ford furnished him with a list of corrections, adjuring him to insert them when he made a new edition.[1] Nearly all the corrections of Ford's list were embodied in the fourth octavo. The title-page of the first volume describes this as 'The Second Edition', which it was not. The title-page of the second volume describes it as 'The Second Edition, Corrected'. Perhaps this distinctive honour was reserved for the second volume because by far the greater number of the Ford corrections appear in it. Ford's list also comments severely upon Motte's editorial falsifications of longer passages, without, however, supplying him with true readings.

Ford's letter, together with the list of minor corrections, was the outcome of dissatisfaction expressed by Swift almost as soon as he received

[1] For the list of corrections see *Gulliver's Travels*, ed. Harold Williams, pp. 423–31.

Motte's volumes. Within three or four weeks of their coming to hand he wrote to Pope:

'I read the book over, and in the second volume observed several passages which appear to be patched and altered, and the style of a different sort, unless I am mistaken....Let me add, that if I were Gulliver's friend, I would desire all my acquaintance to give out that his copy was basely mangled and abused, and added to, and blotted out by the printer; for so to me it seems, in the second volume particularly.'[1]

Our search is for Swift's manuscript. With the two editions of 1727 Motte seems to have satisfied the public demand. We learn from Swift and Ford that there had been conspicuous editorial tampering with the copy; but all that Motte's latest, and revised, text offered, was the adoption of about one hundred literal and verbal corrections. In effect we have learned very little.

Thus matters stood for over five years until in December 1732 Swift announced to Motte that Dublin booksellers were projecting a collected edition of 'all they think to be mine, and print them by subscription, which I will neither encourage nor oppose'.[2] The plan developed into a proposal by George Faulkner, the leading Dublin bookseller of the day, to publish an edition of the Dean's works in four volumes. As the project went forward Swift's

---

[1] *Corresp.* iii, 367–8.   [2] *Ib.* iv, 367.

anxiety that the text of *Gulliver's Travels*, which was to appear as Vol. iii of the collected *Works*, should reproduce the original manuscript became increasingly apparent. He assumed that the manuscript supplied to Motte was no longer in existence, or that it could not be extracted from the London printinghouse, for, writing to Ford, 9 October 1733,[1] he asked particularly for 'a Gulliver interleaved and set right in those mangled and murdered Pages', which he believed Ford to possess or to know of the whereabouts. He had been erroneously informed that Pilkington, a young clergyman, had it; or that it was 'in Mr Corbet's hands'.[2] In answer to inquiry Corbet only sent 'a loose Paper with very little except literall corrections' in Ford's hand. Swift continues:

'I wish you would please let me know, whether You have such an interleaved Gulliver; and where and how I could get [it]; For to say the truth I cannot with patience endure that mingld and mangled manner, as it came from Mottes hands; and it will be extreme difficult for me to correct it by any other means.'

In just under a month, 6 November 1733, Ford replied. His words call for exact attention:

'I lent Mr. Corbet that paper to correct his Gulliver by; and it was from it that I mended my

---

[1] *Letters of Swif to Ford*, pp. 152–5.
[2] Franc s Corbet, Prebendary of St Patrick's.

own. There is every single alteration from the original copy; and the printed book abounds with all those errors, which should be avoided in the new edition.

In my book the blank leaves were wrong placed, so that there are perpetual references backwards and forwards, and it is more difficult to be understood than the paper; but I will try to get one of the second edition, which is much more correct than the first, and transcribe all the alterations more clearly.'[1]

In the Victoria and Albert Museum, South Kensington, will be found the list of corrections prepared by Ford for the use of Motte in his next edition, to which reference has already been made; and there is also an interleaved copy of *Gulliver* with minor corrections noted in the margins and major corrections of the 'corrupted' passages written out in full on the blank leaves in Ford's hand.

Before continuing it should here be noted that there are two copies of the printed work with cor-rections by Ford on blank leaves and minor correc-tions on the text leaves, that at South Kensington, and another in the Pierpont Morgan Library, New York. The two do not wholly correspond, although the corrections, so far as they go, are nearly identical. The South Kensington copy, which is more complete, has about fifty corrections on the face of the printed page additional to those of Ford's

[1] *Letters of Swift to Ford*, p. 156.

list, and seven pairs of blank leaves, all in Vol. ii. On seven of the fourteen interleaves Ford has written out his major corrections. The Pierpont Morgan *Gulliver* is a large paper copy of the first edition. Vol. i has a few corrections in Ford's hand. Vol. ii has four manuscript leaves inserted, and shows many corrections on the text pages. Ford's writing in this copy is closer and he gets more on a page. The South Kensington copy answers to the description given by Ford that 'the blank leaves were wrong placed, so that there are perpetual references backwards and forwards'. This copy was obtained by John Forster from Booth, the bookseller, who purchased it at the Malone sale. It may, therefore, be surmised that it came from Ireland.

The obvious questions which here arise are: (*a*) Is the list of corrections now in the Forster Collection, Victoria and Albert Museum, the document sent to Motte with the use of which he corrected the 1727 edition of *Gulliver*, or is it a draft copy? (*b*) Is this the list which Ford lent to Corbet, or did he send Corbet another 'Paper'?

(*a*) It will be well, before considering the first question, to give the text of Ford's letter, covering the list, in full:

Dublin Jan. 3. 1726[7]

'Sir

I bought here Captⁿ Gulliver's Travels, publish'd by you, both because I heard much Talk of it, and because of a Rumor, that a Friend of mine is suspected to be the Author. I have read the Book twice over with great Care, as well as great Pleasure, & am sorry to tell you it abounds with many gross Errors of the Press, whereof I have sent you as many as I could find, with the Corrections of them as the plain Sense must lead, and I hope you will insert them when you make another Edition.

I have an entire Respect for the Memory of the late Queen, and am always pleas'd when others shew the same: but that Paragraph relating to her looks so very much beside the Purpose that I cannot think it to have been written by the same Author. I wish you & your Friends would consider it, and let it be left out in the next Edition. For it is plainly false in Fact, since all the World knows that the Queen during her whole Reign governed by one first Minister or other. Neither do I find the Author to be any where given to Flattery, or indeed very favourable to any Prince or Minister whatsoever.

These things I let you know out of perfect good will to the Author and yourself, and I hope you will understand me, who am,

Sr your affectionate Friend & Servant
Cha: Ford.'

Although Swift's chief complaint was a wholesale tampering with certain passages the list confines itself to literal and verbal errors, with an occasional comment on corrupted pages. The letter, further, makes special mention of one passage, which, as edited by Motte, exasperated Swift, the table of contents to chapter vi of Part iv, where we read that Gulliver continued to give his Houyhnhnm master a further account 'of the State of England, so well governed by a Queen as to need no first Minister', whereas, as Ford writes, it was notorious that Queen Anne 'during her whole Reign governed by one first Minister or other'.

Is the Forster Collection list that actually handled by Motte? There is evidence that it was, for a time, in other hands than Ford's; and that it was marked by someone not best pleased with the contents. Comments upon passages or pages to which exception is taken are either underscored or struck through. It is difficult to believe that these marks could have been made by Ford himself, for they serve no purpose to the writer of the letter. If the marks were made by Motte, or by someone in his office, the differentiation between underlining and scoring out calls for explanation. The more caustic criticisms seem to meet with harsher treatment. 'False and silly, infallibly not the same Author' is deleted with a single line, whereas two lines are struck through 'manifestly most barbarously cor-rupted, full of Flatnesses,' while 'seems to have much of the Author's manner of thinking, but in many places wants his Spirit' is merely underlined.

I think we may reasonably take it that the Forster Collection list was used by Motte; and, after use, it may probably have been returned to Ford.

(*b*) If so, was it the 'Paper' later lent to Corbet and passed on to Swift? Two very different descriptions of this 'Paper' have come down to us. Swift writing to Ford, 9 October 1733, says: 'On my writing to him [Corbet], he sent a loose Paper with very little except literall corrections in your hand.'[1] Ford in his reply, 6 November 1733, says: 'I lent Mr Corbet that paper to correct his Gulliver by; and it was from it that I mended my own. There is every single alteration from the original copy; and the printed book abounds with all those errors.'[2] What are we to make of Ford's statements that the 'Paper' contained 'every single alteration from the original copy', that he used it 'to correct his Gulliver by', and, further, that he would try to get a copy of 'the second edition, which is much more correct than the first, and transcribe all the alterations more clearly'? It is impossible to re-concile these statements with the facts as we know them; and Ford's description of the 'Paper' he lent to Corbet, as containing 'every single alteration from the original copy', is in direct conflict with Swift's description of the same paper as listing 'very little except literall corrections'. Further-more, Ford professes his intention of trying to get a copy of the 'second edition', by which he meant the octavo of 1727, 'which is much more correct

[1] *Letters of Swift to Ford*, pp. 154–5.
[2] *Ib.* p. 156.

27

than the first, and transcribe all the alterations more clearly'. As we have seen, however, the 1727 octavo embodied only the minor corrections of the list. Why then does Ford say that he hoped to make use of it to transcribe 'all the corrections', which were 'difficult to be understood' owing to the wrong placing of the blank leaves in his copy? The 1727 octavo could be of no service in this respect; for no major alterations were made in its text. Ford was writing seven years after he had addressed himself to Motte in criticism of the faulty text of *Gulliver's Travels*. His memory was indistinct, and he wrote confusedly.

Professor Case,[1] on the strength of Ford's description of the 'Paper' he lent to Corbet, takes to task those, including Dr Hubbard and myself,[2] who assume that Ford's list sent to Motte and the 'Paper' lent to Corbet were identical, or, at least, virtually so in content. He writes: 'It is clear that his "paper", now unfortunately lost, was closer to the original manuscript than either the "list" he sent to Motte or his own annotated copy of the first edition.' This extraordinary statement can only have been due to a mental black-out. Swift, who had seen the 'Paper' within a few weeks of

---

[1] *Four Essays on 'Gulliver's Travels'*, p. 7.
[2] *Contributions towards a Bibliography of Gulliver's Travels*, pp. 52, 53, etc.; H. Williams, *Gulliver's Travels*, p. xlvii.

Ford's letter of 6 November 1733, complained that it contained 'very little except literall corrections' and asked for the 'interleaved Gulliver.' to enable him to provide Faulkner with a true text of the work. In the face of this Case's confident assumption that the 'Paper' was a more complete document than the 'List' and the 'Book' combined is astonishing and incomprehensible. As we have already seen the 'List' is marked by a hand most unlikely, in all appearance, to have been that of Ford himself, and quite possibly that of Motte or someone in his printing-house; and Swift's description of the 'Paper' lent to Corbet leaves little doubt that it was identical with, or very closely similar in content to, the 'List'. Furthermore, if the 'Paper' differed from the 'List', if it offered, as Case assumes, the best means of restoring *Gulliver* to conformity with the original manuscript, why was it lost and when? On Case's assumption it had actually been in Swift's hands at the very time when he was anxious to provide Faulkner with an authoritative basis for establishing the true text of the work. How could a document so important disappear, and apparently just when it was most wanted? If it was inadvertently lost how are we to explain the fact that in subsequent letters of Swift, of Ford, and of Faulkner, there is no mention of the tragedy? There is no evidence to warrant belief in the existence of this document at any time, or of its loss. Furthermore, when we turn to Faulkner's edition of the *Travels* it is quite clear that its revised text is not to be explained by a single intention.

It is at this point that I must pass to consideration of Professor Case's manifesto in favour of the recension *he* adopts in preference to the text of 1735, which was printed in Dublin with Swift's cognizance at the very least, and indeed indisputably with his assistance, the degree of that assistance alone being in doubt.

II. SWIFT'S PART IN THE REVISION OF THE 1735 TEXT OF *GULLIVER'S TRAVELS*

'Gulliver vexeth me more than any' wrote Swift at a time when he was contemplating the new edition of his collected *Works* projected by George Faulkner, the Dublin printer. Vexation still attends both the text of the book and its interpretation. With the interpretation of *Gulliver*, a problem neither textual nor bibliographical, we are not concerned. Whether in Lilliput the Minister Reldresal should be identified with Townshend, Stanhope, or Carteret; whether in the same part of the narrative Skyresh Bolgolam, 'Admiral of the Realm', who was pleased, 'without any provoca-tion' to be Gulliver's 'mortal enemy', stood for the Earl of Nottingham or the Duke of Argyle; whether in the third part the 'great Lord, whose name was Munodi', represents Midleton or Oxford; whether, or not, in the fourth voyage, Swift identified the Yahoos with mankind in general; whether the narrative is dictated by a despairing misanthropy, or whether its purport is to show to what excellencies man can reach if he will but be guided by reason; these questions do not here enter

31

for discussion. In this lecture I wish to occupy myself, in the main and in broad outline, with the important question of the text of *Gulliver's Travels*. We know that Swift was exasperated, genuinely disturbed in mind, by the liberties Motte took with the manuscript, not merely because he disliked seeing his work exposed to the arbitrary mercies of an editor, but because the deletions and alterations distorted his intention and made nonsense of his meaning. We have already seen that he was particularly incensed by an alteration which represented him as declaring that Queen Anne governed without a First Minister, a statement which was 'plainly false in Fact'. Further major alterations either removed altogether, or weakened, satirical passages reflecting on persons, politics, the law, and social life. These changes were, as we have seen, in the first instance adversely commented upon by Ford in his 'List', and later put to rights in his interleaved book.

There are three factors which have to be taken into account in any discussion of the text of *Gulliver*: (*a*) Ford's 'List'; (*b*) his interleaved book; (*c*) Faulkner's edition of *Gulliver*. To these may be added, and here we must be cautious, corrections a modern editor may make, rectifying, for example, obvious mistakes in number and in dates, for these do occur.

No editor will contest the need to restore to *Gulliver*, as first published by Motte, the minor and major corrections of Ford. Faulkner's edition, however, contains further changes. The question which arises is—How far are we to accept these as carrying Swift's direct or indirect authority? In 1938 Professor Case belittled the part Swift was likely to have played in forwarding Faulkner's venture, asserting that Motte's edition was incomparably the soundest basis upon which to build Ford's corrections and enlargements. Nevertheless, Dr Herbert Davis, in 1941, was sufficiently convinced of Faulkner's claims to recognition as to adopt his text in Vol. xi of the Shakespeare Head edition of Swift's *Prose Works*.

There are two printed texts of *Gulliver*, an earlier and a later, separated from each other by an interval of nine years. The later version has some five hundred verbal or minor variants from Motte's earliest text, and, in addition, major alterations, including several lengthy passages. Many of these changes are necessary for mending the sense, for clearing ambiguities, or they are improvements in grammar or style, or they are to be preferred on other general grounds. A proportion might have been made by any intelligent editor. On the other hand those variants which definitely suggest the hand of an author revising his own work are too many to be passed over lightly. At the same time, and I wish to emphasize this point, for it has not been well appreciated, Swift's early complaints upon the appearance of Motte's edition, and the sense of his letters while Faulkner's edition was in course of production, indicate no more than a desire to get back to the original manuscript, not to seize an opportunity which presented itself to effect revision. It may, however, be surmised with some degree of confidence that Ford's 'List' and 'Book' had already been directed to a small measure of revision, passing beyond mere restoration of the manuscript, or the correction of arbitrary changes made by the printer. The substitutions of the interleaved volume (although on this point it is impossible to speak with certainty) have the appearance of going beyond the rectification of passages omitted or altered by Motte. We do not know how thorough Ford's work was, how far he covered departures from the manuscript handed to the printer, to what extent he confined himself to those corrupted passages by which Swift was most aggrieved. Nevertheless, it cannot be disputed that Motte's version, with Ford's corrections and supplemented by the restorations of his interleaved book, presents as near an approximation as we can hope for to the manuscript delivered to the printer. The additional changes of Faulkner's edition were an afterthought, and his text is a revision.

So far agreement is possible, and there is no need to enter into argument with Professor Case. But he goes much further. His conclusion, reached after, let it be admitted, close and laborious examination of variant readings, must be quoted in full.

' The 1735 text, then, is a composite and relatively untrustworthy piece of editing. It is true that a number of its variant readings may have come from Swift's pen, but it is impossible to identify them. It is also true that many of the other intentional variants were made by Swift's general permission. This, however, is beside the point. In law *qui facit per alium facit per se*, but not in literature. The text of 1726 as amended by Ford's careful comparison with the original manuscript, on the other hand, is universally agreed to be as close as is humanly possible to the book as its author intended it to be at the close of a six-year period of inspired creation and detailed revision. It is incomparably the best basis for a text of *Gulliver's Travels*.'[1]

Professor Case sums up with fervour for his client, and has no hesitation in using phrases which put the worst complexion on Faulkner. The manuscript Motte received was the culmination of six years 'of inspired creation and detailed revision'; Ford's amendments represented 'careful comparison with the original manuscript'; the text of 1735, even admitting Swift's recognition and

[1] *Four Essays on 'Gulliver's Travels'*, p. 49.

assistance, was, at the best, an 'untrustworthy piece of editing'. Before we pass to some major considerations which tell against a summing-up so severe, it will be proper to estimate briefly the true weight of these three assertions.

(1) The manuscript Motte received was, we are told, the work of six years ' of inspired creation and detailed revision', the tendentious implication being that any subsequent alterations must detract from the purity and worth of the text. The book collector may prefer to possess a first edition, how-ever faulty the text, but an author's last revision must, as a rule, claim precedence in literature; and Case does not dispute some part played by Swift in the changes which appeared in 1735.

(2) Ford's amendments, so we are told, were the outcome of 'careful comparison with the original manuscript'. That he appears to have taken some care may be admitted, but from what we know of Ford's character it is unlikely that he exercised scrupulous exactness. Further, it is not improbable, and some of Ford's major 'restorations' suggest it, that Swift took the opportunity of criticism by friends, and by others, as reported to him,[1] to introduce modifications of the original. For this we have no direct evidence; but neither have we of the degree, or completeness, of the care taken by Ford.

[1] *Corresp.* iii, 359–60, 367–9.

36

(3) Faulkner's volume is dismissed as 'an untrustworthy piece of editing'. Case's contention here is, in the main, directed to references in Swift's letters and in statements by Faulkner himself to the part friends are supposed to have played in revising the text of *Gulliver*. It will be found, however, that the allusions upon which Case relies have only a limited relevance to that work.

It will now be proper to follow the correspondence with care and consider the pertinent references at some length. On 8 July 1733 Swift wrote to Pope:

'As for the printing of my things going on here, it is an evil I cannot prevent....Some friends correct the errors, and now and then I look on them for a minute or two.'[1]

Faulkner's project was not a new edition of *Gulliver*, but a collection of Swift's writings in four volumes. Swift refers to 'my things', that is the pamphlets and verses which constitute the major part of the publication with which Faulkner was occupied. These presented problems of text and of authenticity, for London booksellers had attributed to Swift many pieces which were not his. Over a year later, 30 August 1734, Swift makes particular mention of the distaste he entertained for false attributions and his anxiety to prevent their inclusion in the forthcoming *Works*. He had let

[1] *Corresp.* v, 1.

Faulkner know 'that if he should publish anything offensive or unworthy, as mine, he should have cause to repent it'. Further, he informs Lord Oxford that the printer had received from friends 'several copies' of 'things ascribed' to him, and that he had ordered 'certain things to be struck out after they were printed'.[1] On 12 May 1735, after the publication of Faulkner's volumes, he told Pulteney that: 'The printer applied to my friends and got many things from England. The man was civil and humble, but I had no dealings with him, and therefore he consulted some friends, who were readier to direct him than I desired they should.'[2] The pretence that he had little or 'no dealings' with Faulkner was maintained by Swift throughout preparation for publication and after, and must be taken with a substantial discount, for the volumes themselves, as we shall see, provide evidence to the contrary. In any event, in this letter Swift had in mind 'many things', not his major writings. Letters to Lord Oxford and to Motte belonging to the same year, repeat the story that friends procured copies for Faulkner, advised, and directed him.[3] Throughout these proceedings Swift asserted that, if only the booksellers in London could come to an agreement, he would have preferred to see his 'things' printed there; but six months later, writing

[1] *Corresp.* v, 85.   [2] *Ib.* v, 180.
[3] 2 September, 1 November 1735; *Corresp.* v, 224, 257.

again to Motte, he made it plain that in any war between the printers he was on the side of Dublin. He regarded it as an 'absolute oppression' that whereas the London booksellers loaded the Dublin market, Irish printers were at a disadvantage. 'If I', he writes, 'were a bookseller in this town, I would use all the safe means to reprint London books, and run them to any town in England'. Later in the same letter he continues: 'For my own part, although I have no power anywhere, I will do the best offices I can to countenance Mr Faulkner; for, although I was not at all pleased to have that collection printed here, yet none of my friends advised me to be angry with him.'[1]

It will be seen that these repetitive statements in Swift's letters, with the story that his friends obtained material for Faulkner and assisted him with advice, concern themselves with the minor works. It is true that Swift, primarily anxious that no spurious pieces should be included, did not spare much labour over the arrangement of his lesser writings, although, as we shall see later, he revised their text carefully. Lord Orrery, Swift's first biographer, writing only about six years after the Dean's death, says:

'Faulkner's edition, at least the four first volumes of it (for there are now eight) were published, by

---

[1]   25 May 1736; *Corresp.* v, 338–40.

the permission and connivance, if not by the particular appointment of the Dean himself.... The four first volumes were published by subscription, and every sheet of them was brought to the Dean for his revisal and correction....In the publication of the six first volumes, the situation and arrangement of each particular piece, in verse and prose, was left entirely to the editor. In that point, the Dean could not, or would not give the least assistance.'[1]

This passage from Orrery is closely related in tenor with Faulkner's claims for his own work. It is clear that he had been put upon his honour to exercise restraint in statement. In the preface to his first volume he says: 'This is all we have been allowed to prefix as a general Preface.' Whenever in this preface Swift is referred to he is 'the supposed Author'. We are told that the 'supposed Author' was persuaded to permit publication of his collected writings by the arguments of his friends 'who were pleased to correct many gross Errors, and strike out some very injudicious Interpolations; particularly in the Voyages of Captain Gulliver...the supposed Author was prevailed on to suffer some Friends to review and correct the Sheets after they were printed, and sometimes he condescended, as we have heard, to give them his own Opinion'. On the title-page of Vol. iii, that is *Gulliver's Travels*,

[1] *Remarks on the Life and Writings of Dr Jonathan Swift* (1752), pp. 79–82.

appears the modest assertion that 'In this Impression several Errors in the *London* and *Dublin* editions are corrected', which, on any showing, can only be characterized as an understatement. In the brief 'Advertisement' of the publisher, prefixed to this volume, the advantage of using [Ford's] inter-leaved book is claimed:

'We are assured, that the Copy sent to the Book-seller in London, was a Transcript of the Original, which Original being in the Possession of a very worthy Gentleman in London, and a most intimate Friend of the Authors; after he had bought the Book in Sheets, and compared it with the Originals, bound it up with blank Leaves, and made those Corrections, which the Reader will find in our Edition. For, the same Gentleman did us the Favour to let us transcribe his Corrections.'

There the matter rested till 1744, when Faulkner, indignant at being accused of piratical practices, printed a statement in his *Dublin Journal* (2 October 1744) claiming that Swift not only consented to the publication of 'a complete collection of his works', but that 'in order to have them appear in the most accurate manner, the Author was pleased to revise every Proof Sheet before it was put to the Press'.

In a preface 'To the Reader', appearing in his later editions, Faulkner stated that the first move came from 'several of the Dean's Friends', who, dissatisfied with the three volumes of *Miscellanies in Prose and Verse*, 1727, edited by Pope, but made up largely from Swift's writings, applied to 'the Editor [Faulkner], to solicit the Author to give him his entire Works to print, free from the Mixture of others'. After some demur Swift consented on condition that 'the Editor should attend him early every Morning, or when most convenient, to read to him, that the Sounds might strike the Ear, as well as the Sense the Understanding'. Faulkner, in doubt whether so strange a proceeding would convince the average reader, including ourselves, proceeded to add:

'Not satisfied with this Preparation for the Press, he corrected every Sheet of the first seven Volumes that were published in his Life Time, desiring the Editor to write Notes, being much younger than the Dean, acquainted with most of the Transactions of his Life, as well as with those of several of his Friends.'[1]

Case's comment upon all this is a remarkable example of special pleading. Faulkner's testimony is dismissed because 'it was made by a man sixty-five years of age, nearly thirty-five years after the events it purported to describe'.[2] The detail of events so important in his life could hardly have been lost to Faulkner's memory whatever his age.

[1] *Works*, vol. i (1762), 18mo edition.
[2] *Four Essays*, p. 18.

The statement he issued in the *Dublin Journal* that
Swift's friends, dissatisfied with the *Miscellanies*,
urged him to undertake a collected edition of the
Works and that Swift revised the proofs,[1] corre-
sponds exactly with his preface to later editions.
Further, in 1744, Faulkner was little over forty.[2]
He was writing nine years only after the publication
of the 1735 volumes, and within the lifetime of
Swift, although, admittedly, after the decay of his
faculties. Even so he was courting question or
contradiction by friends of Swift acquainted with
the course of events before publication. Lord
Orrery's very explicit account, published eight
years later, fully supports Faulkner's claims. In
continuation Professor Case further misrepresents
what happened. The Dublin printer's assertion of
direct assistance from Swift was, we are told,
'made in self-interest as the last shot in a war with
another publisher who had goaded Faulkner for
thirteen years before eliciting this reply'. It was
not a last shot; the statement was made years before
Bathurst's London edition of Swift's *Works* in

[1] Swift himself, about three years after the publication of
the 1735 volumes, writing to Faulkner (8 March 1738),
shows that he was receiving and correcting proofs of his
Polite Conversation, then in course of publication. *Corresp.*
vi, 67–8.
[2] The *D.N.B.* gives 1699? as the year of Faulkner's birth;
but Faulkner, writing to John Nichols in 1774, gives his own
age as 72. Nichols, *Literary Anecdotes*, iii, 208.

1755; it was repeated later; and statements made in self-interest are not thereby discredited. 'It is inconsistent', Case maintains, 'with Faulkner's own account in his original edition.' It is inconsistent only in so far as Faulkner makes it plain (and says as much) that he was not allowed to speak out. He could only refer to Swift as 'the supposed Author', although every reader was conscious of the absurdity.

We must pass on to a strange misapprehension on Case's part. 'The statements of Orrery and Faulkner', he says, 'suggest that among the various friends who assisted Swift in preparing the 1735 edition one was sufficiently predominant to be regarded as "the editor".' He then proceeds to make conjectures among Swift's friends. In his *Dictionary* Dr Johnson's first definition of the meaning of the word 'Editor' is 'Publisher'; and in that sense it was in constant use. Orrery, referring to 'the editor' meant Faulkner; and in his later prefaces Faulkner frequently uses the word to denote himself. In a footnote to the 1756 *Gulliver* he speaks of 'George Faulkner the Editor'. So anxious was Case to minimize the part played by Swift in revision or assistance that he seized upon every opportunity for suggesting that such revision as there was must be largely attributable to friends; and, proceeding a step further, he proposed that in all probability Swift, standing aside, deputed the work of editor-in-chief to a single friend. Carried away by his theory he assigned to the word 'editor' a meaning in which Faulkner and his contemporaries were not using it.

There is no need to question Faulkner's statement that the proposal for a collected edition of the Dean's writings originated in the dissatisfaction of Swift's friends with the content and arrangement of the Pope and Swift *Miscellanies* of 1727. It is found even in Faulkner's first guarded preface of 1735; it was repeated in the *Dublin Journal* of 1744; and thereafter it appeared in later editions of the *Works*. It carries, further, all the evidence of probability, for Pope's editing of these miscellany volumes, despite the warm ties of friendship, gave no pleasure to Swift, nor was it likely to appeal to close friends. The extracts from letters written by Swift in 1733, 1734, and 1735, which have been quoted, confirm the interest of friends in assisting Faulkner, but always the emphasis is upon minor and miscellaneous writings. Faulkner, it is true, does say in his first preface to the *Works*, as we have already learned, that the Dean's friends 'were pleased to correct many gross Errors, and strike out some very injudicious Interpolations; particularly in the Voyages of Captain Gulliver'. Naturally, for *Gulliver* vexed Swift 'more than any', and he took special pains to see that the printer was furnished with Ford's corrections and restorations.

45

I have been trying to show that a major short-coming of Professor Case's thesis is that, his mind directed to a single book, he misleads the reader into supposing that the text of *Gulliver* is an independent problem, obscuring the very important fact that it is only one volume of a set. Before, however, turning to the set as a whole it will be well to examine Case's disposal of a new preface to the *Gulliver* volume of 1735. That it was written by Swift no one questions. If so it must be read as a testimony of approval which cannot be ignored. Case, therefore, in order, once more, to detract from the value of Faulkner's version, suggests that the preface, though written by Swift, was not written for Faulkner. The preliminaries to the Faulkner volume consist of a brief publisher's 'Advertise-ment', the new preface, headed 'A Letter from Capt. Gulliver to his Cousin Sympson', running to nearly six pages, and 'The Publisher to the Reader', which had already appeared in Motte's edition. In his 'Letter' Captain Gulliver chides Sympson for the excisions and insertions he has permitted in the text of the *Travels*. He then passes on to repent his own 'great Want of Judgment' in consenting to the publication of his papers, prevailed upon as he was by the hope that they might exercise a salutary moral influence, whereas after six months he cannot learn that the 'Book hath produced one single Effect' for good. He then returns to complain of

46

confusions in the text, to amend which he sends
'some Corrections', although, as he learns that
'the original Manuscript' is all destroyed, he finds
it difficult to adjust everything as he would wish.
After touching on other matters he concludes with
abandoning all hope of reforming the Yahoo race:
'I have now done with all such visionary Schemes
for ever.'

The 'Letter' is dated '*April* 2. 1727', which
would be just over five instead of 'after above six
Months' since the first publication. Swift was
rarely accurate in stating dates. Later, in the same
'Letter', he speaks of 'seven Months'. Despite the
dating of the 'Letter' it can scarcely be doubted that
it was written expressly for Faulkner. It is
specifically referred to by Faulkner in his 'Advertisement'. He begins: 'Mr. Sympson's Letter to
Captain Gulliver, prefixed to this Volume, will
make a long Advertisement unnecessary.' The odd
mistake, which seems not to have been noted before,
that he speaks of the 'Letter' as addressed by
Sympson to Gulliver, and not, as it should be, by
Gulliver to Sympson, may have been due to haste
while the preliminaries were being set up to ensure
early publication. In any event the tenor of his
allusion shows that he regarded the 'Letter' as a
new and special contribution to his volume. Case,
however, maintains that it was probably written
at the time of its date and for Motte; and that it is

logically a postscript rather than a preface. In effect it may be a postscript to Motte's editions, and would be so if written in 1727. Faulkner's 'Advertisement', however, describes it as designedly 'prefixed' to his edition. It is quite incredible that if it had been sent to Motte in 1727 he would, in 1735, have been ready to surrender it to a rival publisher. To meet this difficulty Case suggests that, although the 'Letter' was written in 1727, it may never have been sent to Motte; or, if sent, Swift had preserved a copy. These are assumptions for which no evidence is forthcoming. He further suggests that the Gulliver 'Letter' to Sympson resembles in content and in phraseology Ford's letter to Motte of 3 January 1727 covering the list of corrections. The only resemblance is inherent in the subject, the errors of Motte's edition, especially the statement which galled Swift that Queen Anne governed without a First Minister. Furthermore, we know that on 27 April 1727, under the fictitious name of Sympson he was negotiating a financial settlement with Motte.[1] This seems to rule out any likelihood of his having written for Motte, little more than three weeks earlier, so important a letter as that prefixed to Faulkner's *Gulliver*.[2] I regard also, as an added argument of weight, the fact that in a miscellaneous volume of Swift manuscripts preserved

[1] *Corresp.* iii, 386.
[2] Hubbard, *op. cit.* p. 76; Williams, *Gulliver*, pp. xlii–xliv.

in the Forster Collection, South Kensington, is to be found a paper containing in Swift's hand, together with scraps of Anglo-Latin *jeu d'esprit*, a sentence which appears in the 'Letter'. These trifles he frequently exchanged with his friends in the seventeen-thirties. The trial sentence, therefore, was probably jotted down about 1734 rather than in 1727.[1] Furthermore, no small part of Gulliver's 'Letter' is directed to emphasizing the importance of the *meaning* of the printed narrative of travel and the examples for public good which it contains. This emphasis is much more likely in retrospect and prefatory to a new edition. Finally, the fictitious date is all in keeping with the mystification Swift was fond of practising in connexion with verse or prose pamphlets. If, as seems almost certain, the 'Letter' was written in 1734, or 1735, it lends additional authority to Faulkner's edition. Case's anxiety to disparage that edition would naturally prompt him to cast suspicion upon the 'Letter'.

In a spoken lecture it would be presumptuous to expect an audience, wherever found, tolerant of the attempt to present a complete textual collation of variant readings running through a work as large as *Gulliver's Travels*. It is possible, however, to advance general evidence in favour of Faulkner's text independently of lengthy tabulations of variants,

[1] First noted by me in the *Times Literary Supplement*, 10 January 1929.

confirming his claims and leaving us in little doubt that he was a frank and honest man, if not particularly perspicuous or gifted with a quick eye to detect faults for himself. Even if we make deductions from what may be some exaggeration in his own favour, there is nothing which cannot be reconciled with his earlier preface, nor any measure of improbability sufficient to make us question his sincerity. As we have seen he asserts in the 'Advertisement' to his first edition that he had the advantage of using a corrected and interleaved book. Now Ford's book was a copy of Motte's first edition, not the fourth octavo of 1727, and there can be no doubt that Faulkner, if we disregard the manuscript corrections and restitutions, was setting up from a first edition. Motte's revised fourth octavo was definitely not lying before him.[1] In addition to the restitutions of the blank leaves Ford noted in his book (with the exception of three verbal or literal corrections) all the errata which appeared on his list, and he marked further minor corrections on the printed page. The number of minor corrections runs in all to nearly 150. Of these about one hundred are adopted exactly in Faulkner's text, and a few more with slight modification. In about twenty instances stylistic reasons, or the usage of his

[1] Readings peculiar to Motte's 1727 octavo are not adopted by Faulkner; it is clear, therefore, that this edition was not before him when he was preparing his text.

printing-house, led him to follow Motte's printed text in preference to the changes made by Ford. In other instances Ford's corrections are needless, debatable, or for the worse. It may be surmised, further, that the compositor failed to notice a few slight corrections. On the evidence we may assume, with reasonable confidence, that Ford's book, now in the Forster Collection, was placed in Faulkner's hands.

In seventeen instances Ford, in his book, altered the older possessive 'mine', in such phrases as 'mine eyes', or 'mine ears', to 'my'. These changes were not adopted by Faulkner, possibly, as Case suggests, because Swift intended to represent Gulliver as a plain man, old-fashioned in ways, thought, and speech. Two preferences, indicative of Swift's practice, may next be noted. In his letters he shows a liking for 'hath' in place of the more modern third person singular 'has'. The Dublin *Gulliver* has a tendency to the same usage. In the 1735 text 'though' is changed to 'although' at least twenty-two times. It is, therefore, parti-cularly noteworthy that in his own copy of the *Miscellanies*, 1727–32, Swift, with his pen, twenty-five times altered 'tho'', or 'though' to 'although'.[1] His clearly marked preference for

---

[1] On the other hand, for some reason not easy to divine, Swift was content in the text of one tract, *Sentiments of a Church of England Man*, to correct 'tho'' to 'though' seven times and four times 'though' to 'although'.

'although' was governed by ear. He chose, in general, the euphony of 'although', especially in sentence contexts where it gave better tone modulation. Another change, not so much in evidence, but apparent, may be attributed to the printing-house. About a dozen times the monosyllable 'till' becomes 'until'. This change was never marked in the prose portion of the *Miscellanies*; and, as likely as not, the compositor was responsible for the few examples which appear in Faulkner's text. This probability is strongly borne out by a comparison of the posthumously published London and Dublin editions of Swift's *Four Last Years of the Queen*, 1758. In this work Millar, the London bookseller, practically always uses the monosyllable 'till', whereas Faulkner, as constantly, has 'until'. Swift spent years in preparing this work for the press, and it is unlikely that so marked a contrast distinguished two manuscripts over which he had supervision. The differentiation belongs to the two printing-houses.

As has been noted, therefore, confining the summary for the present to Ford's minor corrections, two-thirds were adopted by Faulkner without change, a few were slightly modified, and Swift's stylistic preferences can, with some confidence, be judged to have influenced the disregard of a fair proportion of the remainder. Thus we are not only entitled to believe that the corrections of Ford's book lay before Faulkner, but more, and this is important, we are provided with evidence that Swift's hand can be detected in the 1735 text.

The seven pairs of blank leaves in Ford's book are all in Vol. ii, which contains the voyages to Laputa and the land of the Houyhnhnms. On these blank leaves Ford has written out longer corrections, or restitutions, of the passages mangled or perverted by the London editor. These, if Motte ever saw them, find no place in the revised text of his fourth octavo, 1727. It remains to see how Faulkner made use of them. The first passage to be noted is of interest in the evidence it provides of independent as contrasted with slavish following. The superior excellence of Laputan telescopes is described in chapter iii of Part iii. We are told that the astro-nomers of the Flying Island observed the 'celestial Bodies' with instruments of an excellence enabling them to extend their discoveries far beyond 'Astronomers in Europe'. Here Ford introduces a sentence stating that

'although their largest Telescopes do not exceed three Feet, they magnify much more than those of an hundred Yards among us, and at the same time shew the Stars with greater Clearness'.

Faulkner modifies this addition to

'than those of a Hundred with us, and shew the Stars with greater Clearness'.

Motte had contented himself with the bare statement that Laputan instruments were better. The
change shows an editorial hand, almost certainly
Swift's; and Faulkner's reading is clearly an
improvement. It has been said that a telescope one
hundred yards long lay beyond the imagination of
the eighteenth century. This is not altogether true.
Part iii contains many references to contemporary
events between 1720 and 1725. In 1722 James
Bradley, who had recently been appointed to the
Savilian Chair of Astronomy at Oxford, measured
the diameter of Venus with a tubeless instrument
212 feet long. Ford's 'an hundred Yards' might,
however, as a general statement, be regarded as
excessive. Such an instrument *was* unknown.
Faulkner reduced the measure to 100 feet, half the
length of Bradley's tubeless telescope, and therefore
readily within conception. We can hardly question
that Ford was restoring, whether accurately or
not, a passage in the manuscript which Motte
omitted in the belief that it embodied absurd
exaggeration. It is probable that Swift had
Bradley's telescope in mind, an instrument which
was in use while he was writing *Gulliver's Travels*;
and that, in 1735, when revision was possible, he
reduced Ford's scale of comparison to more
reasonable proportions. Furthermore, he struck
out the unnecessary words 'at the same time',
which appear in Ford's correction. It may seem

54

that I have lingered too long over a few words;
but, so far as I know, no previous commentator
has mentioned Bradley's telescope, and the passage
as a whole is singularly suggestive of the author
himself engaged on the minutiae of revision.

In the same chapter of Part iii Ford's book
provided for a lengthy insertion, which was, however, so clearly an allegory of the successful
opposition to Wood's halfpence, that Faulkner
discreetly refrained from introducing any part of it
into his text for fear of arousing the displeasure of
the government. This, it may be observed, is a
passage which should be restored in any recon-
structed text of *Gulliver*.

In chapter vi of Part iii Ford struck out a long
passage, pp. 90–3, treating of plots against the
State and the methods adopted by decipherers of
secret papers, substituting a more vigorous version
of the same topic. Motte, for fear of offending the
authorities, had toned down the passage. Faulkner
followed Ford with a few variations, on the whole
lending still further force to the satire. In addition
to these changes, suggestive of the author's hand,
there are two small alterations almost certainly
made by Swift himself. In one instance, by the
substitution of 'how' for 'that', Faulkner avoided
tautology, a disfigurement of style we know to have
been peculiarly distasteful to Swift; and Ford's
'has' becomes 'hath', following a practice he

55

preferred. Unfortunately, if Swift was responsible for the latter change, it escaped his notice (as Professor Case pointed out) that it failed to comply with the accompanying anagram.

In the Table of Contents appearing in the first edition before Part iv of the Voyage to the Houyhnhnms, the entry for chapter vi read:

'*A Continuation of the State of* England; *so well governed by a Queen as to need no first Minister. The Character of such an one in some* European *Courts.*'

Chapter vi was headed with the same words. It will be remembered that Ford in his letter of complaint to Motte, 3 January 1727, took particular exception to this entry. In his book he corrected it to

'*A Continuation of the State of* England. *The Character of* a first Minister.'

Faulkner added the words '*under Queen* Anne' after 'England', and '*in the Courts of* Europe' after 'Minister'. The second addition can readily be explained as dictated by caution, lest the savage satire should be read as a direct attack on Walpole; but why a far from attractive picture of social life in England should be assigned to the reign of Queen Anne is difficult to explain. It looks as if Faulkner was responsible here for additions which are in conflict with one another.

In chapter v of Part iv there is a passage describing Princes in 'many *Northern* Parts of *Europe*', who maintain themselves by hiring out mercenary troops. Ford altered the location of these Princes to 'Germany and other *Northern* Parts of *Europe*'. This was too much for Faulkner who, with a Hanoverian dynasty on the throne, did not dare to mention Germany, contenting himself with the reading of the first edition.

In the same chapter, pp. 69–79, Gulliver gives his Houyhnhnm master a lengthy description of the law, lawyers, and the administration of justice 'according to the present Practice' in his own country, in plain matter-of-fact terms which clothe the satire with an icy bitterness. In an allusion to this passage in his list Ford told Motte: 'You ought in Justice to restore those twelve Pages to the true Reading.' He described them as: 'Towards the end &c. manifestly most barbarously corrupted, full of Flatnesses, cant Words, and Softenings unworthy the Dignity, Spirit, Candour, & Frankness of the Author.' On the presumption that Ford's version in the book does represent the manuscript Motte received, it can only be said that whoever altered the copy for Motte took a great deal of trouble and must, if the compositor was to follow him at all, have rewritten a large portion of the textual content of these pages. In addition to lesser verbal changes the reviser altered the sequence of paragraphs, and greatly extended the length of the matter with a loose verbiage which disfigures the style and weakens the force of the satire. Faulkner follows Ford with a few verbal variations; and these, if anything, for the better.

The heading of chapter vi, Part iv, is changed in conformity with the table of contents, as noticed already, to correct the absurdity of describing Queen Anne as governing without a 'first Minister'. Here the reviser for Motte introduced a lengthy laudatory account of administration by 'our She Governor or Queen' for which Ford substituted a few lines descriptive of the character of 'a first or *chief Minister of State*', who is 'a Creature wholly exempt from Joy and Grief, Love and Hatred'. Faulkner followed Ford with two slight differences.

Near the end of the same chapter is a paragraph reflecting upon the physical and mental imperfections of the nobility and people of quality. This was abbreviated and toned down by Motte. Faulkner has three verbal variants from Ford. In each instance the changes are an improvement.

The only conclusion to be drawn from these textual collations is that Faulkner follows so closely the corrections of Ford's book, both minor and major, that the statement in the 'Advertisement' to his edition can scarcely be called in question. He made use of the corrected work now resting in the Forster Library, or a copy of the book indistinguishable in character. He restored the 'sting' to most of the passages, which, as altered by Motte, formed the chief ground of Swift's complaints. In some instances, however, timidity restrained him from going as far as Ford. Furthermore, we can claim that there are very distinct indications in Faulkner's text of word forms preferred by Swift himself.

I can only deal here briefly with Case's lists of textual variants as between Motte and Faulkner.[1] These lists are divided into sections: 'variant readings which involve differences of meaning; variants concerned with grammar and idiom; and purely stylistic variants.' A fair proportion of the readings which first appear in the 1735 edition are, beyond question, improvements in one or other of these categories, and are so admitted to be by Case himself. He is, further, prepared to recognize that Faulkner's text displays a sprinkling of what are obviously compositor's oversights, or misprints chargeable only to faulty proof-reading, in no way a criterion of judgement between one text and the other. When we come to variants for which he asserts that the 1726 readings are preferable, or to debatable emendations, we enter the field of opinion, and I hold that although it may be conceded that Faulkner's text sometimes goes astray, occasionally makes a change for the worse, or

[1] *Four Essays on 'Gulliver's Travels'*, pp. 21–48.

misses the point of a passage, equally it cannot be denied that a large proportion of Faulkner's readings are manifest improvements. Furthermore, Case's comments are sometimes pedantic.

The external evidence for Swift's supervisory interest in the 1735 edition of *Gulliver's Travels* is supported, if with characteristic aloofness, by his letters, by contemporary statement, and by the publisher. Many textual changes bear distinctive marks of Swift's style and idiom. Whatever evidence there is for any part played by Swift's friends is related, in the main, to the selection of lesser writings which were to be included in the other volumes projected by Faulkner. The striking fact is that in these volumes the evidence against Case's contention gathers weight. He allowed preoccupation with *Gulliver* to obscure the fact that it is only one volume of a set, and cannot be treated independently. The other volumes betray marked revision attributable to the author and to no one else. Lord Rothschild possesses a set of the Pope and Swift *Miscellanies in Prose and Verse*, 1727–32, with corrections in the hand of Swift. Most of these corrections and revisions were adopted by Faulkner when reprinting miscellany pieces in his own volumes. Further revision in these volumes can hardly, on internal evidence, be ascribed to any one but to Swift himself. Professor Case has much to explain, confining himself to *Gulliver's Travels* only. The evidence against him accumulates if we turn to the further volumes published by Faulkner. An edited text based on the first edition can hardly assert preference.

I propose to consider in my next lecture the character and content of the *Miscellanies* of 1727–32, for the editing of which Pope was responsible; Swift's manuscript corrections of his own pieces in these volumes; the reflection of these changes in Faulkner; and, further, textual corrections in Faulkner additional to Swift's manuscript annotations.

This survey, providing demonstrative proof of Swift's interest in Faulkner's first, second, and fourth volumes, supplies contributory evidence, which cannot be gainsaid, for his constant oversight of the third volume, *Gulliver's Travels*.

III. SWIFT'S
AUTOGRAPH CORRECTIONS OF THE
MISCELLANIES, 1727–32

The publication of miscellany volumes, containing
contributions in verse, or in prose, or in both, by
two, three, or more authors, began early, not so
many years after the invention of printing, and has
continued into our own day. The use of the word
'miscellany' is no longer, apparently, much in
favour; and the sixteenth century chose happier
titles. Could we but now select from the publishers'
lists a new *Handefull of pleasant delites* or *The
Paradise of Daintie Devises* or *Englands Helicon*,
how much greater our expectancy when the book
arrived and we began to turn its pages! The gift
for inventing these and the like titles passed with
the end of the century, and we come to less
imaginative descriptions. The seventeenth century
was peculiarly rich in votive volumes, *Funebria
Sacra*, or *Lacrymae*; thence we pass, by contrast,
to *Wits Recreations*, or *Merry Drollery* and,
towards the end of the century we come upon
the uninformative *A Collection of Poems by Several
Hands*; and a little later came *Miscellany Poems*,
the first of the six collections, 1684–1709, commonly

known as Dryden's, or otherwise Tonson's, *Mis-cellanies*. The pattern and the title came into being together; and in the first half of the eighteenth century the words 'miscellany', 'miscellanies', or 'miscellaneous' are of constant recurrence. In the first fifty years of the century generalized collections approximately matched in number those of the preceding two centuries.

The student of the earlier part of the eighteenth century will soon become aware of the important part played during this period by the many miscellany volumes published. Leading poets of the time made their first appearance in print in one or other of these collections. It has been said, and rightly, that 'a knowledge of the more important miscellanies of the period is essential to any one who is to attempt to edit an eighteenth-century poet, and to establish the canon of his work'.[1] It is no part of my duty to comment further on these miscellanies in general. They vary in the quality of their content; but there are few in which we shall not find a poem or two by an anonymous or forgotten writer which will amply reward us for pages of indifferent verse. In these books we come upon the first printings of poems by Pope, Swift, Prior, Gay, Lady Winchelsea, it may be in versions afterwards revised by the author. The outstanding example is

[1] Iolo A. Williams, 'Some Poetical Miscellanies of the Early Eighteenth Century', *The Library* (Dec. 1929), x, 233.

Lintott's miscellany of 1712 in which appeared the earlier version of Pope's *Rape of the Lock* in two cantos only. By contrast with miscellanies distinguished by contributions from famous authors the two volumes of *Miscellaneous Poems, By Several Hands. Published by D. Lewis*, 1726, 1730, deserve mention. Few of the verses are by more notable hands, all are published anonymously, the merit of the contents is considerable, and for every one of us in this (and in other miscellanies) a pleasant pastime may be found in the search for untraced authors, some of whom, in Lewis's miscellany, are claimants for the best of the pieces garnered by him.

The most important, however, of the miscellaneous collections brought together in the earlier half of the eighteenth century were the four volumes of *Miscellanies in Prose and Verse*, 1727–32, edited by Pope. These volumes are not strictly comparable with the general miscellanies of the time. They are almost completely dominated by two authors, and so meant to be. The first volume, wholly in prose, has only one piece not by Swift; nearly two-thirds of the second volume, also consisting of prose, came from Arbuthnot, the rest from either Pope (with a possible qualification in one instance) or from Swift; the third volume, described on the title-page as 'The Last', had one prose piece, which was written by Pope; twenty out of the seventy or so verse pieces were also written by him, whereas nearly all the rest were Swift's; the fourth volume, that of 1732, confusingly designated 'The Third', has a prose section divided between Pope, Swift, and two or three others, while in a count of pages the verse portion falls largely to Swift. It was this volume which chiefly dissatisfied him. It will be remembered that while Faulkner was projecting his edition of the *Works* Swift's friends were also concerned to remedy the arrangement for which Pope was responsible, and to exclude doubtful pieces.

Pope was credited with having his own advantage chiefly in mind in the course of editing the *Miscel-lanies*, calling upon Swift for as much as he could extract, and withholding as much as he decently could of his own work for publication elsewhere. Thomas Sheridan, referring to Swift's visit to England in 1727, puts the case thus:

'It was then that Pope published his Volumes of Miscellanies, consisting of some of his own Works, and Arbuthnot's, but chiefly of select Pieces of Swift's. As this was the first time that any of his Works were printed collectively, the sale was immense, and produced a considerable sum to Pope, who had the whole profit, as Swift was at all times above making any pecuniary advantage of his writings.'[1]

Swift also suspected that Pope had not wholly acted the part of a friend in furnishing out the

[1] *Life of Swift*, 1784, p. 250.

content of the 'Third' volume. He complained in a letter to Motte that he was very dissatisfied with the whole publication, for he discovered that while 'six-sevenths of the whole verse part'[1] was his, the verses were largely trifles. Later, writing again to Motte, he says: 'My part, which in the verses is seven-eighths, is very incorrect.'[2]

Sheridan's implication that there was little to be found in the *Miscellanies* except 'select Pieces of Swift's' is misleading. In the first volume, it is true, only fifteen pages out of 408 were not written by Swift; but in the second volume, running to 358 pages, his contribution extended to no more than twenty-six pages. The 'Last', counting prose and verse together, was a volume of 455 pages, of which 243 were Swift's.[3] In the first three volumes, therefore, Swift's part (661 out of 1229 pages) was more than half, but by no means overwhelmingly preponderant.[4]

The 'Third' volume, 1732, stands apart. The prose portion consists of 276 pages, of which 84 are covered by Swift. In making this calculation I reject two small pieces, *The Wonderful Wonder*

---

[1] *Corresp.* iv, 359–61; 4 Nov. 1732.

[2] *Ib.* iv, 367; 9 Dec. 1732.

[3] Swift wrote on the recto of the first blank leaf in his copy of the 'Last' volume, '252 Pages of one Author'.

[4] Dr Teerink's statement of Swift's part in the three volumes is misleading. *The History of John Bull*, for example, was not written by Swift.

66

of Wonders, and *The Wonder of all the Wonders*, which have been attributed to him; but both on internal and external evidence I consider them more than doubtful. It is noteworthy, for example, that whereas Pope grouped all Swift's other contributions together he placed these two much earlier in the volume. The verse portion of the book extends to exactly one hundred pages, of which eighty-seven are Swift's. His statements, therefore, that 'six-sevenths', or in another place 'seven-eighths', of the verses were his are singularly near the mark.

He has two further complaints—that these pieces were only 'humorous or satirical trifles' and that they were 'very incorrect'. That they were mere trifles is not true. Some of his best pieces appear—*The Journal of a Modern Lady, The Country Life, Mary the Cook-Maid's Letter, Dr. Swift to Mr. Pope, A Soldier and a Scholar*—not to name others. Are they incorrect? This is a question worth examining. The poems, ten in number, must be taken one by one. *The Journal of a Modern Lady* first appeared as a carelessly printed Dublin pamphlet, 1729, entitled *The Journal of a Dublin Lady*, and thereafter three or four times before it was included in the *Miscellanies*. On its first appearance Swift, writing to Ford, described it as 'printed all into nonsense'[1]. This is a complete exaggeration. There are some verbal errors, due

[1] *Letters of Swift to Ford*, pp. 130–1.

apparently to the compositor's difficulty in reading the manuscript; but in his own copy of the *Miscellanies* Swift contented himself with making ten verbal alterations, only two or three of which are of any significance. *The Country Life*, when first published in 1721 as a broadside, carried the title of *The Journal*. In the miscellany volume lines 3–6 were omitted, presumably because of the personal allusions to two of Swift's friends, Sheridan and Delany. These lines Swift did not restore; he corrected one mis-spelled word, and marked six further changes of a minor character. In *On Cutting down the Old Thorn at Market Hill* he marked three verbal changes, which are improvements, but not essential. In *A Pastoral Dialogue* he merely deleted a duplicated word. Against *Mary the Cook-Maid's Letter*, which was first printed in this miscellany volume, no correction appears. *Mad Mullinix and Timothy* was first printed in 1728 as a Dublin pamphlet. Although Swift, writing to Pope, described the pamphlet as 'very incorrect'[1] he penned only three small corrections of the 1732 text. A few changes look like improvements by Pope, who was also, probably, responsible for the deletion of lines 25–34 as too coarse. The *Epigram on seeing a Worthy Prelate go out of Church* is unmarked by Swift, as is also *Dr. Swift to Mr. Pope. A Soldier and a Scholar*

[1] *Corresp.* iv, 308; 12 June 1732.

appeared simultaneously, January 1731–2, under different titles and in differing versions, in London and Dublin.[1] When printed in the 1732 miscellany the English text was followed. In his copy of the book Swift added four lines and made one verbal correction. His seven markings for italics or verbal corrections against *To Doctor D——l——y on the Libels writ against him* present no changes of importance. He also added a footnote.

If we are to judge the inaccuracy of the text of these ten poems by Swift's manuscript corrections, we can only say that in describing them as 'very incorrect' he was using exaggerated language. He had every opportunity, with the volume in his hands, to make extensive corrections, but the sum total amounts to little. I have, in the first instance, paid special regard to the verse section of the last miscellany volume edited by Pope because Swift directed against it what major complaints he had to make.

At the close of my second lecture I stated my intention of examining how far Faulkner transferred to his text of the 1735 *Works* corrections made by Swift himself in the miscellany volumes, on the ground that *Gulliver's Travels* could only be regarded as one volume of a set, and that the

---

[1] It should be added in passing that the poem survives in Swift's holograph, in the possession of Lord Rothschild. This manuscript preserves the Irish text as printed by Faulkner.

reflection of the author's corrections in the first, second, and fourth of Faulkner's volumes must lend greater authority to readings peculiar to the third volume, that is *Gulliver*, even if these sometimes appear needless or scarcely to be counted improvements. It will be convenient, therefore, before we retrace our steps, to ask how far the poems we have been examining show, as printed by Faulkner, signs of deference to Swift's manuscript corrections. The answer is that of the thirty-one corrections made by Swift twenty-four, that is four-fifths, were adopted by Faulkner.[1] It is specially remarkable, further, that although Faulkner reprinted *A Soldier and a Scholar* under the title he used for his Irish version of the poem, *The Grand Question Debated*, following its text also with some revision, he included the four additional lines supplied by Swift in the *Miscellanies*. It looks as if he had that corrected volume lying before him.

In the light of this conjecture, but with an open mind, it will now be proper to turn back to the beginning and examine the earlier volumes of the *Miscellanies* to discover to what extent Faulkner's 1735 text reflects Swift's manuscript corrections.

It must not be supposed from what has been said about Swift's irritation with the 1732 volume that

[1] Faulkner did not include *Mad Mullinix and Timothy* in his 1735 volumes.

disagreement between the friends arose from the beginning, or that Pope, as an editor, was arbitrary and careless. In the publication of his own writings Pope was wont to exercise constant care, and he would not be less meticulous if entrusted with the writings of a friend for whom, of all his con-temporaries, he held the highest regard. The joint project was a venture arrived at during Swift's visit to England in 1726. As soon as he was back in Dublin he began to select suitable pieces for inclusion in the *Miscellanies*. As early as 15 October we find him writing to Pope:

'I am mustering, as I told you, all the little things in verse that I think may be safely printed, but I give you despotic power to tear as many as you please.'[1]

Pope busied himself at once with the disposition of the pieces in their respective volumes; and the printer responded promptly. In a letter addressed to Swift on 18 February of the following year he was able to report:

'Our Miscellany is now quite printed. I am prodigiously pleased with this joint volume, in which methinks we look like friends, side by side.... The third volume consists of verses, but I would choose to print none but such as have some peculiarity, and may be distinguished for ours, from other writers.'[2]

[1] *Corresp.* iii, 349.   [2] *Ib.* iii, 380.

71

Volumes i and ii were published on 24 June 1727; the 'Last' volume on 7 March of the following year, 1728. It will be seen from the dates that Pope's reference to 'this joint volume' applied to the first and second volumes. When Swift was again in England in 1727 he wrote to Sheridan from Twickenham on 1 July:

'Pray copy out the verses I writ to Stella on her collecting my verses, and send them to me, for we want some to make our poetical Miscellany large enough, and I am not there to pick what should be added.'[1]

The design at this time was that the 'Last' volume should consist of miscellaneous poems by Pope and Swift. While Swift, during the summer, was staying at Twickenham with his friend, Pope was industriously at work on *The Dunciad*, for it was intended that it should appear in this forthcoming volume. The poem, however, was outgrowing Pope's earlier thoughts, and at the end of June he wrote to Motte that 'it will make three sheets at least, and I will take time till winter to finish it. It may then be published singly first if proper'.[2] In the upshot *The Dunciad* did appear 'singly', in May 1728, about two months after the publication of the miscellany volume, in which, to fill out the book, Pope inserted at the beginning his prose attack on

[1] *Corresp.* iii, 403.
[2] *Pope's Works*, Elwin and Courthope, ix, 524.

dunces, ΠΕΡΙ ΒΑΘΟΥΣ: *or...The Art of Sinking in Poetry*. His purpose was something much more than a mere substitution or make-weight. If, as he presumed it would, *The Art of Sinking in Poetry*, served to arouse angry rejoinders from his victims, he would enjoy a better advantage in the retaliatory thrusts of his poem. Yet another piece found its way into the volume on doubtful grounds—Swift's longest poem, *Cadenus and Vanessa*; for this, like the ΠΕΡΙ ΒΑΘΟΥΣ, has its own separate register and pagination. Another curious fact is that, despite doubts of inclusion which appear to have attached to *Cadenus and Vanessa*, the poem was already in print as early as June 1727. In the letter which Pope addressed to Motte, referred to above, he says: ' Send me next (after the sheet R and this) the last sheet of Cadenus and Vanessa...let them print one half sheet for me of the beginning of Cadenus.' It was on 1 July, the very day following this missive, that Swift wrote to Sheridan the letter, also referred to above, requesting more verses ' to make our poetical Miscellany large enough'. The allusion to sheet R is puzzling, for, as the volume now stands, two poems of Swift's complete and portions of two others occupy these eight leaves. Pope originally intended that *The Dunciad* should appear in this volume. This, even in the unexpanded form it had reached when it first appeared as a separate publication, would have furnished out a miscellany volume comparable in size with its predecessors. By the time Swift wrote to Sheridan Pope *had* abandoned the thought of including *The Dunciad*, but only with the set purpose of baiting the dunces with the prose ΠΕΡΙ ΒΑΘΟΥΣ. Then, for some reason, *Cadenus and Vanessa*, which hung in doubt, was included, and the third miscellany volume emerged as considerably the largest of the three, as well as a bibliographical curiosity. A strange feature of *Cadenus*, further indicating hesitant procedure, is that the last page of sheet A is numbered 8 and the first page of the next sheet is numbered 17, although there is no gap in the text, and pagination thereafter continues normally to the end of the poem.

While these indecisions were delaying the arrangement of the various pieces to be included in *The Last Volume* Swift left London, on 18 September, for his return to Ireland. The verse transcripts for which he had written to Sheridan had not, apparently, reached Twickenham before he left. A group of six poems by Swift, separated from earlier contributions, conclude the volume. Of these the last but three is the address to Stella upon her collecting and transcribing his poems. This it was that Swift had asked for particularly; and we may suppose that Sheridan had been slow in carrying out his office. That conjecture is much strengthened by the last poem but one, *To Stella*,

Visiting me in my Sickness, to which the quite impossible date, '*October*, 1727' was assigned, presumably by Pope. Swift, it may be noted, in the letter addressed to Sheridan, requested him to 'Direct them, and all other double papers, to Lord Bathurst, in St. James's Square, London'.[1] The delay may have occurred there. In any event '*October*, 1727' must have been the belated date of receipt, which somehow got printed beneath the title of the poem. At this time Stella was herself suffering from a protracted illness which was to prove fatal in the early part of the next year. She was in no condition to visit Swift, who had, during the whole period of his stay in England, been in constant anxiety about her. Dr John Lyon, who knew Swift intimately, has left a note in his copy of Hawkesworth's *Life of Swift* (Forster Collection, South Kensington, No. 579) stating that the lines were written in 1720, and this, with hardly a doubt, is the correct date. We know that in the earlier part of 1720 Swift was seriously indisposed, suffering from severe attacks of giddiness.

What had happened was that *The Last Volume* was already sufficiently filled out when a batch of six poems by Swift arrived from Ireland, or from Lord Bathurst. Perhaps Pope had, by this time, forgotten about the further accession which was on its way. He could hardly, however, reject these

[1] *Corresp.* iii, 403.

poems, and grouped them at the end of the book, inadvertently allowing a receipt date to masquerade as a date of composition at the head of one piece.

The first volume carries the title *Miscellanies in Prose and Verse*, although it contains no verse; the second volume, also without any verse content, is simply *Miscellanies*; the 'Last' volume, which does contain verse, and was originally intended to be a gathering of miscellaneous poems, is also *Miscellanies*, although a separate title before the verse section bears the words 'Miscellanies in Verse'; and the 'Third' volume, of 1732, although it contains both prose and verse, is *Miscellanies* only. The first volume is introduced by a preface of fourteen pages signed by Swift and Pope, the names in that order, and dated from Twickenham 'May 27. 1727'. As Swift was at this time in England, and Pope's guest, the preface can be accepted as a joint production. Its main purport is the profession, at what may be considered needless and repetitive length, of a compulsion, owing to the many false attributions from which they had suffered, to 'own such Pieces as in our stricter Judgment we would have suppressed for ever' for they represented in truth 'not our Works, but our Idlenesses'. The preface acknowledged further the inclusion of some papers by other hands or written in conjunction with others. It need hardly be remarked that the authors' profession of indifference to the writings they were publishing was a pose not to be taken seriously.

It has been noted that the contents of the first volume were all in prose, and, with a single exception, all written by Swift. His own copy of this volume is heavily corrected, the manuscript markings numbering not much less than three hundred. I now turn to examine how far Faulkner's 1735 text was influenced by Swift's emendations in this, the first volume of the miscellany set.

His first prose pamphlet, *Contests and Dissentions between the Nobles and Commons in Athens and Rome*, published in 1701, drew a parallel with the contemporary political scene. It appears as the first piece in the miscellany and in Faulkner's Vol. i, in the one instance covering eighty-six pages, in the other fifty-five. Swift's corrections, eighty-six in number, that is an average of one for every page of the miscellany, are almost all of a minor nature—mis-spellings, changes in punctuation, substitutions of 'it is' for ''tis', of 'although' for 'tho'', of 'hath' for 'has', together with a few improvements in grammar or phrase. It is remarkable, therefore, that Faulkner followed all but eight of the changes.

Next, both in the *Miscellanies* and in Faulkner, comes *The Sentiments of a Church of England Man*. Here the rate has increased. In fifty-three pages eighty corrections are marked. Of these twenty-one were not adopted by Faulkner; but all Swift's markings, except four or five, are directed to punctuation—commas where none were and decidedly were not wanted, or semicolons for colons, and the like. Indeed, the sprinkling and strengthening of punctuation was overdone by Swift, and the compositor, if he had the book before him, did wisely in passing over much of it. For the rest he followed the emendations with almost consistent faithfulness.

An Argument against abolishing Christianity follows. With few exceptions Swift's corrections, fortyfive in number, are matters of pointing or spelling. Only nine are not adopted by Faulkner's compositor, and two of the emendations have been subjected to later revision. There are only seven corrections against *A Project for the Advancement of Religion*, and Faulkner follows five. For *A Letter concerning the Sacramental Test*, which comes next in the *Miscellanies*, we have to turn to Faulkner's fourth volume. Of about thirty corrections twothirds are followed in Faulkner's text; but more significant is the fact that in the margin Swift marked two pages for omission, and these are duly omitted. There are only two corrections in *A Tritical Essay upon the Faculties of the Mind*, rectifying definite verbal inaccuracies, and Faulkner makes the necessary changes. Thereafter in the last 148 pages of the first volume of the *Miscellanies*, containing the Bickerstaff papers and other pieces,

Swift's corrections are few and desultory. It is clear, however, that at the least, he glanced over these pages, although there was no systematic attempt to make even necessary emendations. Each correction, ten in number, is, however, followed by Faulkner. Three were mere mis-spellings; and the context would have suggested to any compositor 'Boy' for 'Body' and 'Conquests' for 'Contests'.

In the Second and 'Last' volumes there was, in prose, only one piece by Swift, *A Letter to a Young Lady*, and this is unmarked.

Consideration has already been given to Swift's corrections of the verse portion of the 1732 volume, called the 'Third'; and we have noted that, in the main, these were followed by Faulkner. Prior place was given to an examination of these poems because Swift had particularly described them as 'incorrect'. This volume also contains four prose pieces which were certainly written by Swift, and, in addition, two which have been attributed to him. Each of these has been marked by someone, in pencil, with the symbol of a pointing hand, as have, it may be noted in passing, those poems in the same volume which were written by Swift. Who was responsible for this marginal marking it is now impossible to say. Swift himself is hardly to be suspected, for the rough touch is not suggestive of him, and his other markings were in ink. Four of the six prose essays in the volume, *A Modest*

Proposal for Preventing the Children of the Poor in Ireland from being a Burden to their Parents, *A Vindication of Lord Carteret*, *An Essay on the Fates of Clergymen*, and *An Essay on Modern Education* are undoubtedly by Swift. A doubt may be entertained about the other two, *The Wonderful Wonder of Wonders* and *The Wonder of All the Wonders*. In style and humour these two pieces fall much below what might be expected of him; they were placed by Pope separately from Swift's other contributions; and there is some evidence for Sheridan's authorship. In a letter addressed to Knightley Chetwode, 13 March 1721–2, Swift wrote, after reference to a distasteful publication by 'one Dobbs a surgeon', that 'Mr. Sheridan's hand sometimes entertains the world, and I pay for all'.[1] Was the reference to these two pieces? The date falls correctly. Dr Herbert Davis, in Vol. ix of his edition of Swift's *Prose Works*, now in progress, though impressed by the evidence for Swift's authorship, consigns these writings with commendable discretion to an appendix.[2]

The four tracts indubitably by Swift, occupying eighty-four pages, are only marked in sixteen places. A cross in the margin against words which make nonsense, receives attention, and the remaining alterations are adopted by Faulkner.

[1] *Corresp.* iii, 125.
[2] *Prose Works of Jonathan Swift*, ix, pp. xvii, 281–7.

Only one section of the 1727–32 *Miscellanies* now remains to be studied in collating Swift's corrections against the 1735 text—the verse portion of the 'Last' volume so-called; and this occupies by far the greater part of the book. Thirty-six of the poems are by Swift. Manuscript notes and corrections in Swift's own copy of the volume number, however, no more than twenty.[1] These are corrections of simple and obvious errors, minor rephrasings, brief notes, or identifications of persons named. Faulkner follows the changes in general, and takes cognizance of those calling for no definite alterations. He has, further, many additional changes from the text of the 1727 volumes, which, it is clear, he was using as copy when setting up his own volumes. These variants are, in the main, verbal and of no major importance; but they do suggest the hand of an author. In treating of those changes in the text of the Faulkner edition of *Gulliver's Travels* for which there was no warrant in Ford's list or in his book Professor Case argued that Swift's supervision was 'perfunctory', and that many of these alterations were the work of his friends. It will, I think, be readily admitted that in verse, as contrasted with prose narrative, it is more than

[1] In his own copy of Faulkner's Vol. ii, 1737, Swift marked these same poems half a dozen times. These corrections were, of course, made after the publication of the Dublin 1735 set of four volumes.

unlikely that an author would be prepared to see his lines tampered with, nor is it easy to believe that a friend would assume so invidious a responsibility. Swift had complained of the incorrectness of some of his published poems. This shows that he had strong feelings on the subject. If it is difficult to believe that major changes came from any hand but Swift's we may fairly conclude that the verbal changes were also his. *A City Shower*, one of the poems included in the 'Last' volume, has in Faulkner, in addition to a few slight literal and pointing amendments, a remodelled couplet. For

> 'His only Coat, where Dust confus'd with Rain
> Roughen the Nap, and leave a mingled Stain'.

he reads,

> 'Sole Coat, where Dust cemented by the Rain
> Erects the Nap, and leaves a cloudy Stain.'

Surely this, pictorially, in versification, and, it may be added, in grammar, is an author's improvement?

Take another poem, which, like that just cited, was unmarked by Swift in his copy of the *Miscellanies*, his imitation of the seventh epistle of the first Book of Horace, addressed to Lord Oxford. Faulkner definitely improves line 60:

> 'Where painted Monsters are hung out,'

by substituting 'dangle out'. Line 133, 'I have Experience dearly bought,' becomes, with advantage

to the emphasis, 'Experience I have....' The last
couplet but one of the poem is remodelled:

> 'But you resolv'd to have your Jest,
> And 'twas a Folly to contest:'

becomes

> 'But it's a Folly to Contest,
> When you resolved to have your Jest.'

This reads like Swift. For one thing he preferred,
as we learn from his manuscript corrections, to see
'it is' for ''tis', or 'it was' for ''twas'.

In printing singly the *Epitaph on a Miser* Pope,
or Swift, picked out part of a poem only. *An Elegy
on Demar* is said to have been composed by Swift
and several friends, including Stella, in company.
The *Epitaph* has most of Swift's manner, and this
may account for the omission in 1727 of the *Elegy*
which leads up to it. Further, it is interesting to note
that these lines which had frequently been printed
before, were revised for inclusion in the *Miscellanies*. Two lines were omitted, the following line
remodelled, and there is, in addition, a verbal change.
Faulkner adopts the revised form of the *Epitaph*.

A poem of singular interest among those included
in the *Miscellanies* is *Atlas*, for not only has a holograph survived,[1] it carries a certificate in Pope's hand:

> 'This is the Original, in Dr. Swift's hand.
>   A. Pope'

[1] Now in the possession of Lord Rothschild.

We would naturally suppose this to be the manuscript used by Pope when he was editing the 1727
volumes; but it is not, for there are six well-defined
variant readings. Here another point of interest
emerges. In the library of the Duke of Bedford
there is preserved a book in which Stella made
transcripts of some of Swift's poems. Among these
we find *Atlas* in exactly the version of Swift's
holograph even to peculiarities of spelling. This
holograph, endorsed by Pope, is probably the very
manuscript from which Stella copied.

The textual history of *The South-Sea*, another
poem included in this miscellany section, is ex-
ceedingly complicated; but the whole need not
here detain us. In December 1720 Swift sent to
Charles Ford in London the manuscript of a poem
on the South-Sea Bubble running to fifty-five four-
line stanzas. Ford made a transcript, gave the poem
the title of 'The Bubble', sent it to the printer, and
it was published early in January 1720/1. The poem
was frequently reprinted before it appeared in the
Miscellanies. In Dublin prints, and in a transcript
made by Stella, two additional stanzas were introduced, making fifty-seven in all. When printed in
the *Miscellanies* the poem was completely revised.
The title was changed to 'The South-Sea', a Latin
quotation heading the poem was removed to the end,
and thirteen of the fifty-seven stanzas were omitted,
although Stella's two additional stanzas were

included. Further, two distinctive new readings were introduced. Swift, as has been said already, was staying with Pope when the miscellany volume was in progress, and these extensive changes must have had his approval. They were probably made on his own initiative, for in his own copy of the book he made no marks against the poem. The abbreviation of the poem is, however, difficult to explain, especially in view of the call for more material and the fact that in Faulkner's volume eleven out of the thirteen rejected stanzas were restored. What plainly appears is Swift's interest in Faulkner's edition. It strains credulity too far to suppose that the poem, as restored in 1735, was not Swift's work.

To proceed. A study of minor changes in Faulkner's text of the 1735 volumes, that is of new readings there introduced for the first time into the poems, still further tends to confirm our faith in revision by the author himself. Swift was constantly upon the look-out for tautology. In lines 86 and 87 of *Cadenus and Vanessa* the word 'Earth' in two successive lines had survived many reprints. Faulkner, in line 86, substituted 'Land'. In line 759 for 'Vanity's the Food of Fools' Faulkner reads 'Flattery's the Food of Fools', a change hardly likely save on the part of the author. In line 823 the substitution of 'act' for earlier readings, 'like' or 'love' is clearly dictated by discretion, and must have come from Swift himself. In *Baucis and*

Philemon Faulkner's text has a sprinkling of innovations definitely improvements metrically or in vigour. In *The Description of a Salamander*, where (lines 11 and 12) in earlier printings hieroglyphs were said 'T' express' valour, strength, or wit, Faulkner, followed by later editors, substituted, more correctly, 'To shew'. In *Pethox the Great*, a poem bearing one manuscript correction by Swift, there are several verbal changes in Faulkner, which, if of no special significance, are thereby only the more likely to be from the author's hand.

To summarize conclusions, at this stage, in so far as they relate to the verse section of *Miscellanies. The Last Volume*. It has been shown that authoritative manuscript corrections made by Swift in his own copy of that book were followed later by Faulkner; that major alterations, rearrangements, and revisions, are difficult to explain except as his work; and that minor corrections, which are few in number, have every appearance of being those of an author and of no one else.

We may safely assume that Swift's notes and corrections in the miscellany volumes were made before Faulkner's publication of the Dean's *Works* in 1735. In all there are, in the four volumes, about 350 pen markings; and most by far of the changes and corrections were adopted in Faulkner's text. If these identical volumes were, in whole or in part, used by the Dublin printer, they were later returned; and sometimes Swift turned over the pages. The poem addressed to Stella, for her birthday, 13 March 1724/5, ends:

'No Length of Time can make you quit
Honour and Virtue, Sense and Wit,
Thus you may still be young to me,
While I can better *hear* than *see*;
Oh, ne'er may Fortune shew her Spight,
To make me *deaf*, and mend my *Sight*.'

The word 'deaf' was underlined by Swift, and in the margin he wrote, 'now deaf 1740'.

I must now turn again from the verse to Swift's prose contributions to the *Miscellanies*. As we have seen already it is in the first volume of the miscellany set that we find most of Swift's prose contributions. The volume is heavily corrected, and only one piece is not by Swift. In the second volume only one piece was written by him, and this is unmarked. In *The Third Volume*, 1732, four prose pieces undoubtedly by Swift are printed. These received little attention from his pen. In considering, therefore, changes in Faulkner's text additional to Swift's manuscript corrections, it is the first volume which chiefly calls for examination.

As has been shown already nearly all Swift's manuscript corrections of the prose pamphlet *Contests and Dissentions*, numbering over eighty in all, were followed in the 1735 text. There are, however, in addition, about fifty variants from the text of the miscellany volume. These are, with four or five exceptions, literal or verbal changes, cor- rections of slips, substitutions of the plural for the singular noun, or the reverse, minor improvements of style, and so forth. Even the few examples of rephrasing are slight in character. These corrections were doubtless made on the face of Faulkner's proofs. It would be rash to deny categorically that some might have been made by Swift's friends; but for the most part they certainly have the appearance of scrutiny by the author. When we have positive proof in his own handwriting of Swift's desire to mend the text, it is hard indeed to believe that, after this trouble, he was ready to allow friends to potter at sweet will with the proofs. We are, of course, any of us who are in the habit of writing books, happy to enlist the help of competent friends. They may spot slips which we have overlooked; they may offer suggestions which we are glad to adopt. But who is prepared to hand over proofs to friends according them full liberty to do what they like and post them on to the printer? Not one of us. Swift was anxious, from what we know of him, that what he wrote should be faithfully printed. Dr Herbert Davis, in the course of textual notes in his edition of Swift's *Prose Works*, says of Faulkner's venture: 'There is...no reason to believe that anything was included in the early volumes of the collected edition published in 1735 of which Swift would not approve.'[1] This statement is certainly supported by all that we have thus far noted, and by the text of the further prose tracts, following upon *Contests and Dissentions*, which were included in the first volume of the *Miscellanies*.

In *The Sentiments of a Church of England Man* there are about twenty-five corrections in the Faulkner text additional to the manuscript changes already indicated by Swift. The remarks which have been made, in discussing further changes in the previous pamphlet, apply again with equal force and propriety. In *An Argument against abolishing Christianity* only nine of Swift's forty-five corrections were not incorporated by the printer. Less than forty further changes appear in the 1735 text. Of these, however, a large proportion, nearly half, are words or phrases italicized in order to emphasize the irony. A few words had already been underlined by Swift in his copy of the *Miscellanies*. We may then believe with assurance that the additional italics also came from him; and this lends contributory evidence of weight in favour of the other changes in the 1735 text. *A Project for the Advancement of Religion* has over forty alterations and corrections appearing for the first time in the 1735 text, although Swift had made very few marks against it in his miscellany volume. There is a major deletion of interest, warranting a special note.

[1] *Prose Works of Jonathan Swift*, ii, 275.

89

Writing of the clergy 'who constantly wear a distinct Habit from others' and of the scandal caused, on occasion, by the unbecoming conduct of some in public places, Swift gave it as his opinion that

'it were infinitely better if all the Clergy (except the Bishops) were permitted to appear like other Men of the graver Sort, unless at those Seasons when they are doing the Business of their Function'.

This passage was struck out in 1735. Evidently, on reconsideration, Swift either doubted the wisdom of his earlier opinion or suspected that it might be open to misconstruction. This is by far the largest alteration in the text of the pamphlet.

As has been noted the most significant emendation of *A Letter concerning the Sacramental Test*, in addition to a fair number of minor corrections, was the deletion of two pages. It was nearly twenty years since this polemical tract had been written. Swift made it clear that the argument still expressed his convictions and was as valid in 1735 as 'when the Discourse first appeared'.[1] Nevertheless, in addition to minor corrections, certain changes were demanded by the passage of time. In the *Miscellanies*, following earlier printings, we find the supposed author, a member of the House of Commons of Ireland, asserting:

'I remember when I was last in *England*, I told the King, that the highest Tories we had

[1] 'The Publisher's Advertisement to the Reader', 1735.

with us, would make tolerable Whigs there; this was certainly right, and still in general continues so, unless you have since admitted new Characteristicks, which did not come within our Definition.'

This passage disappears from Faulkner. The fictitious place of writing, 'Dublin', and the date, 'December *the* 4th, 1708' are removed from the end.

There are few corrections in the latter part of the first miscellany volume. If, however, we look at the Bickerstaff papers, as they appear in Faulkner, we find fairly numerous additional changes, which, in character, bear a strong resemblance to those in-cluded in earlier papers. There are also three notes to these papers, first supplied by Faulkner, which in two instances must be wholly attributable to Swift, and in the third partly so, if garbled at the end. In *A Vindication of Isaac Bickerstaff* the hypothetical author states that 'the *Inquisition* in *Portugal* was pleased to burn my Predictions, and condemn the Author and Readers of them'. A footnote informs the reader:

'This is Fact, as the Author was assured by Sir Paul Methuen.'

A footnote on the next page explains that

'The Quotations here inserted, are in Imitation of Dr. Bentley, in some part of the famous Con-troversy between him and Charles Boyle, Esq; afterwards Earl of Orrery.'

An introductory note to *Predictions for the Year 1708* reads:

'It is said, that the Author, when he had writ the following Paper, and being at a Loss what Name to prefix to it, passing through Long Acre, observed a Sign over a House where a Locksmith dwelt, and found the Name Bickerstaff written under it: Which being a Name somewhat uncommon, he chose to call himself Isaac Bickerstaff.'

The note then refers to the adoption of the name by Steele and Addison in *The Tatler*, in which paper 'as well as many of the *Spectators*, it is well known, that the Author had a considerable Part'. Swift's part in these two papers was, in fact, small. The note may have come from Faulkner himself, but hardly unprompted, and the conclusion may have been a misguided flourish on his part. In any event the two footnotes previously cited are clearly additions by Swift and virtually demonstrative evidence that Faulkner's proofs for this part of the volume lay before him. This conclusion supports the belief that other alterations in the text should be assigned to his oversight.

If we turn now to the last paper in this miscellany volume, *A Letter from a Young Gentleman, Lately enter'd into Holy Orders*, we find, in addition to changes typical of Swift's stylistic practice, a textual alteration, accompanied by a footnote, which, as Dr Herbert Davis observes, is 'a good example of Swift's final revision'.[1] 'Our Education', wrote Swift, 'is so corrupted, that you will hardly find a young Person of Quality with the least Tincture of Knowledge, at the same Time that the Clergy were never more learned.' As he turned over the proofs Swift boggled at this earlier statement. He changed 'Clergy' to 'many of the Clergy', and appended a footnote: 'N.B. This Discourse was written Fourteen Years ago, since which Time, the Case is extremely altered by Deaths and Successions.'

I hope I was successful, in the previous lecture, in making it evident from Swift's letters, from Orrery's comment on Faulkner's volumes, from the statements of Faulkner himself, that if Swift's friends had any part to play in promoting the 1735 edition of the *Works*, it was probably limited to dissatisfaction with Pope as an editor of the *Miscellanies*. The chief grounds of dissatisfaction seem to have been the selection and arrangement, for which Pope was responsible. These two factors appeared to them to mislead the public into crediting the Dean with pieces he had not written. The gravamen was erroneous attributions into which careless arrangement betrayed the unsuspecting reader.

Swift's protestations of the little interest he took in Faulkner's venture, even of unwillingness to countenance it, of his readiness to leave the affair

[1] *Prose Works of Jonathan Swift*, ix, 373.

largely to his friends, were but parts of the disguise behind which throughout life he hid connexion with his own writings. The set of *Miscellanies* corrected in his own hand, which happily has survived, was almost certainly in Faulkner's hands while he was engaged in assembling material for the first four volumes of his edition of the Dean's *Works*. If not, corrections identical with those in the *Miscellanies* were supplied to him. It is easier to believe that he actually held the volumes.

In the text of those writings printed by Faulkner from the *Miscellanies* in his first, second, and fourth volumes, many additional minor changes appear. These, especially in stylistic characteristics, conform to the pattern of Swift's manuscript corrections. There are some changes, including annotations, which can only be attributed to the author himself. There is not, from any correction, alteration, deletion, or addition, any warrant for the supposition that Swift's friends were let loose upon the text, and much to justify a conviction that he himself, very likely in conjunction with Faulkner who furnished him with proofs, was alone responsible for the additional variants.

If this be true of a very considerable part of three of Faulkner's volumes I suggest, to say no more, that it is not unlikely that it should be equally true of his remaining volume, *Gulliver's Travels*.

94

For EU product safety concerns, contact us at Calle de José Abascal, 56–1°,
28003 Madrid, Spain or eugpsr@cambridge.org.

www.ingramcontent.com/pod-product-compliance
Ingram Content Group UK Ltd.
Pitfield, Milton Keynes, MK11 3LW, UK
UKHW012335130625
459647UK00009B/307